CAMPAIGN 260

FORT WILLIAM HENRY 1755–57

A battle, two sieges and bloody massacre

IAN CASTLE

ILLUSTRATED BY GRAHAM TURNER

Series editor Marcus Cowper

First published in Great Britain in 2013 by Osprey Publishing,
PO Box 883, Oxford, OX1 9PL, UK
PO Box 3985, New York, NY 10185-3985, USA
E-mail: info@ospreypublishing.com

A CIP catalogue record for this book is available from the British Library.

ISBN: 978 1 78200 2741
E-book ISBN: 978 1 78200 275 8
E-pub ISBN: 978 1 78200 276 5

Editorial by Ilios Publishing Ltd, Oxford, UK (www.iliospublishing.com)
Index by Rob Munro
Typeset in Myriad Pro and Sabon
Maps by Bounford.com
3D bird's-eye view by The Black Spot
Battlescene illustrations by Graham Turner
Originated by PDQ Media, Bungay, UK
Printed in China through Worldprint Ltd.

14 15 16 17 18   10 9 8 7 6 5 4 3 2 1

DEDICATION

Dedicated to the memory of Colin Spicer (1960–2012)
A good friend, greatly missed.

ACKNOWLEDGEMENTS

I would like to take this opportunity to thank those who have been of
assistance to me during the preparation of this book. I am particularly
grateful to Will Raffle for the time he spent translating large sections of
French text for me and also for compiling the French order of battle for the
Siege of Fort William Henry. I have also had a number of interesting and
useful exchanges with Michael Johnson on matters relating to the Native
Americans and with David Starbuck on the recent archaeological work at
the fort.
At the Fort William Henry Museum I met with an enthusiastic response to
my request for help with illustrations from Melodie Viele and Lauren
Sheridan – despite the freezing temperatures at Lake George at the time! I
am also indebted to Olga Tsapina and Brian Moeller at the Huntington
Library, California, for permission to reproduce General Webb's infamous
letter to Fort William Henry.
Accomplished artists Mark Churms and Gary Zaboly have both generously
allowed me to use pieces of their excellent work and it goes without saying
that I am in awe of Graham Turner for turning my sketchy notes and ideas
into beautiful works of art.
And I also must thank Leslea Barnes and Ryan Gale in America and Xander
Green, Katy Turle-Smith, Steve Vickers and Geoff Ketcher in the UK for
allowing me use of their re-enactment photographs.
Finally, I am grateful to members of New France Old England, the UK's only
French and Indian War re-enactment group, some of who appear in photos
in this book while others have unknowingly 'modelled' for the artwork
plates! For more details of the group go online at www.nfoe.org.uk
Unless otherwise stated photographs used in this book are from my own
collection.

ARTIST'S NOTE

Readers may care to note that the original paintings from which the color
plates in this book were prepared are available for private sale. The
Publishers retain all reproduction copyright whatsoever. All enquiries
should be addressed to:

Graham Turner, PO Box 568, Aylesbury, Bucks, HP17 8ZX, UK
www.studio88.co.uk

The Publishers regret that they can enter into no correspondence upon this
matter.

THE WOODLAND TRUST

Osprey Publishing are supporting the Woodland Trust, the UK's leading
woodland conservation charity, by funding the dedication of trees.

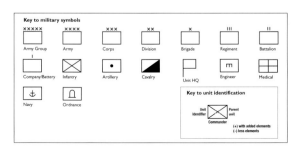

CONTENTS

British planned military operations, 1755

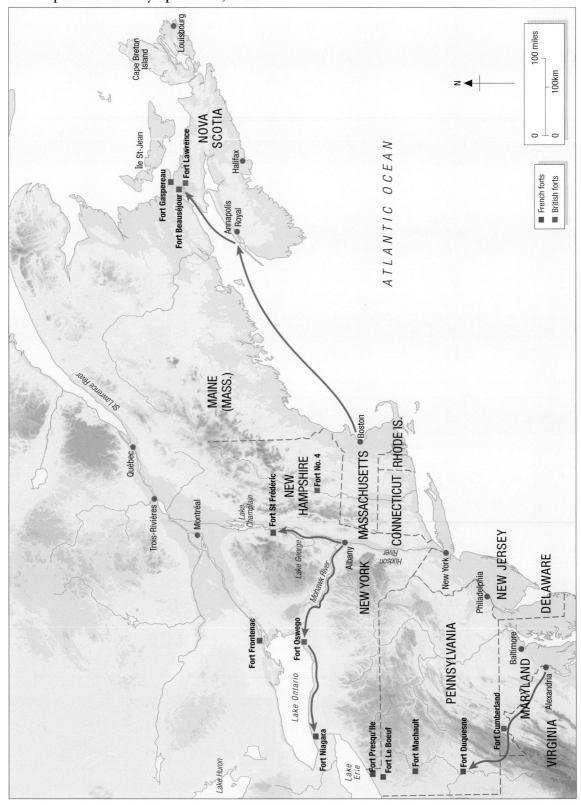

Louisbourg

Cape Breton Island

Île St-Jean

NOVA SCOTIA

Fort Gaspereau
Fort Lawrence
Fort Beauséjour

Halifax

Annapolis Royal

ATLANTIC OCEAN

St Lawrence River

MAINE (MASS.)

Québec

Boston

Trois-Rivières

Montréal

Fort St Frédéric

Fort No. 4

NEW HAMPSHIRE

MASSACHUSETTS

CONNECTICUT

RHODE IS.

Lake Champlain

Lake George

Albany

Mohawk River

Hudson River

New York

NEW JERSEY

DELAWARE

Philadelphia

Fort Frontenac

Fort Oswego

NEW YORK

PENNSYLVANIA

Baltimore

MARYLAND

Alexandria

Lake Ontario

Fort Niagara

Fort Presqu'île
Fort Le Boeuf

Fort Machault

Fort Duquesne

Fort Cumberland

VIRGINIA

Lake Huron

Lake Erie

N

100 miles

100km

0

0

French forts

British forts

INTRODUCTION

When in 1826 James Fenimore Cooper published his classic of American literature, *The Last of the Mohicans*, just 69 years had passed since the siege of Fort William Henry and the infamous massacre of the British garrison. Many of his readers had direct contact with those who lived through this traumatic period of American history. They were as close then as we are today to soldiers who took part in the D-Day landings of 1944. To those people the story he told rang true. By then the British Army was long gone from America's shores but for the former British colonists, now American citizens, the frontier terrors of the mid-18th century still occupied a haunting place in the national psyche. Sensationalist accounts of the siege and massacre were repeated and embellished in the American press, then travelled to London to gain credence when reprinted in the influential city newspapers. Cooper's story relied on this material and reflected the beliefs and values of the time in its portrayal of the almost demonic savagery of the Indian attack on a column of British and colonial soldiers after the capitulation of Fort William Henry. He wrote, 'Death was everywhere, and in his most terrific and disgusting aspects. Resistance only served to inflame the murderers, who inflicted their furious blows long after their victims were beyond the power of their resentment. The flow of blood might be likened to the outbreaking of a torrent.'

James Fenimore Cooper (1789–1851). *The Last of the Mohicans*, published in 1826, became Cooper's most popular work. It was the second novel in a five-book series known collectively as *The Leatherstocking Tales*, published between 1823 and 1841.

It is this version of mass slaughter – a massacre – that dominates subsequent film and television adaptations of the book; it is the one that has achieved common acceptance and forms for many the 'real' story of events that day. The truth is somewhat different.

ORIGINS OF THE FRENCH AND INDIAN WAR

Britain and France both began establishing and strengthening colonies on the North American continent in the 17th century. The French claimed ownership of an immense territory known as New France which extended in a great arc from the Atlantic seaboard at Île Royale (now Cape Breton Island) along the St Lawrence River to the Great Lakes and southwards to New Orleans on the Gulf of Mexico. In most places the only signs of occupation were the small isolated forts established to support New France's important fur trade. Although claiming authority over this vast land, the French population numbered only around 75,000 people. By contrast some 1.5 million settlers populated Britain's 13 colonies, compressed into a stretch of the east coast extending from Nova Scotia in the north to Georgia in the south. With these colonies looking to expand, inevitably the two nations were set on a collision course.

The end of the War of the Austrian Succession in 1748 settled an uneasy peace between Britain and France in Europe, but the war had also extended to America and this settlement did little to ease tensions there. In particular both nations nurtured a desire to control the largely uncharted Ohio River Valley. In 1749 a group of Virginian traders and British businessmen created the Ohio Company to exploit trading opportunities in the region with the intention of later opening up the land for settlement. The French became increasingly concerned about this encroachment which, if it became firmly established, would endanger New France's communications, weaken their influence with the Native Americans in the region and result in a crippling loss of trade. The Iroquois Confederacy also claimed the same region and had for decades preserved a balance by accepting gifts from both Britain and France to maintain diplomatic relations. But now their influence had waned. To make the point that New France considered this territory was theirs, a far-reaching expedition buried lead plates throughout the valleys of the Ohio and Allegheny rivers, officially staking its claim to the land. The British took little notice.

In 1753 tension escalated. The French built three forts linking the Ohio with Lake Erie, Fort Niagara and ultimately Montréal. Robert Dinwiddie, governor of Virginia, delivered an ultimatum demanding French withdrawal. With neither side prepared to step back from the brink a collision became inevitable.

In February 1754 a 40-man company of Virginia militia occupied the 'Forks of the Ohio' – the junction of the Ohio, Allegheny and Monongahela rivers – and began construction of a simple fort. In mid-April, just as they completed work, about 500 French soldiers appeared with artillery. The ensign in command of the militia, faced with the option of immediate surrender or having his makeshift fortification smashed into matchwood, with him in it, accepted the French terms and marched away. The French then built a substantial and imposing fort on the site, which they named Fort Duquesne.

News of this development angered Dinwiddie who ordered a young but ambitious Virginian militia officer, George Washington, to build a road for artillery towards the new French fort. On 24 May, while at Great Meadows, still about 70 miles from Fort Duquesne, Washington received intelligence that a French party had camped nearby. The French carried an ultimatum instructing the British to vacate the territory. Washington ambushed the group on 28 May 1754. For more information on this controversial attack and Washington's subsequent surrender, see Campaign 140: *Monongahela 1754–55* (Osprey Publishing Ltd: Oxford, 2004). Although Britain and France had not officially declared war, the two nations had drawn their swords and many years of savage warfare would pass before they could return them to their scabbards.

CHRONOLOGY

1754

22 December — Major-General Edward Braddock, the new British commander, sails for America.

1755

20 February — Braddock arrives in Virginia.

3 May — The French despatch six battalions to New France under the command of Baron Dieskau.

29 May — Braddock marches from Fort Cumberland towards Fort Duquesne.

16 June — British capture Fort Beauséjour.

Late June — Dieskau arrives at Québec.

Early July — William Johnson forms provincial force in Albany for attack on Fort St Frédéric.

9 July — **The battle of the Monongahela.** Braddock defeated and mortally wounded.

16 July to 17 August — Johnson's command assembles at the Great Carrying Place on Hudson River.

10–20 August — French troops march from Montréal towards Fort St Frédéric on Lake Champlain.

26 August — Johnson moves up to Lac du St Sacrement with part of army.

Late August — Johnson renames Lac du St Sacrement as Lake George.

2 September — Dieskau moves his men to Carillon at the junction of Lake Champlain and Lac du St Sacrement.

3 September — Johnson orders up rest of his force to Lake George.

4 September — Dieskau advances to attack Fort Lyman.

7 September — Dieskau targets the British camp at Lake George instead.

8 September — **The battle of Lake George.** French defeated; Dieskau wounded and captured.

Mid-September — Work starts on a small stockaded fort at Lake George.

Late September — French commence building Fort Carillon.

29 September — Decision taken to build a stronger fort at Lake George.

13 November — Flagstaff raised at new fort, Fort William Henry.

1756

January	John Winslow appointed by William Shirley to command provincial troops in attack on forts Carillon and St Frédéric from William Henry.
March	Lord Loudoun appointed new British commander in North America.
11 March	Marquis de Montcalm selected to replace Dieskau.
12 May	Montcalm arrives at Québec.
18 May	War between Britain and France officially declared (Seven Years War).
7 June	Daniel Webb arrives at New York as interim British commander.
25 June	James Abercromby arrives at Albany and takes over as temporary British commander.
23 July	Lord Loudoun arrives at New York.
14 August	The British forts at Oswego surrender to Montcalm.
20 August	Cancellation of attacks on the French forts at Carillon and St Frédéric.
Winter	The British 44th Regiment garrisons Fort William Henry supported by 100 rangers.

1757

21 January	The battle on Snowshoes.
19–23 March	**First French Siege of Fort William Henry.**
29 March	Lt. Col. George Monro, 35th Regiment, takes command of Fort William Henry.
23 July	Sabbath Day Point massacre.
25–29 July	Brigadier-General Webb inspects Fort William Henry.
3–9 August	**Second Siege of Fort William Henry.**
10 August	Fort William Henry 'massacre'.

OPPOSING COMMANDERS

BRITISH COMMANDERS

William Johnson was born in Ireland around 1714 and travelled to America in early 1738 to develop lands owned by his uncle in the Mohawk Valley in the province of New York. Johnson established himself as a major businessman and built a profitable trading relationship with Mohawk settlements in the region. Having earned the respect of the Mohawks, around 1742 they initiated him into their nation, giving him the name Warraghiyagey, which he explained meant 'A Man who undertakes great Things'. Because of his growing influence amongst the Mohawks and his increasing involvement in public affairs, New York appointed Johnson as Indian Commissioner in 1744. But in 1751, caught up in the jealousies of rival political factions, he resigned. However, following the arrival of Edward Braddock in 1755 as commander-in-chief of the army in North America, Johnson returned to office as the superintendent of Indian affairs. But, perhaps a little more surprisingly considering his lack of military experience, Braddock also appointed him as major-general in the provincial army with instructions to lead a campaign against Fort St Frédéric, a strategically important French post at Crown Point on Lake Champlain. For his subsequent victory at the battle of Lake George he became Sir William Johnson, 1st Baronet of New York. Two years later, in the 1757 campaign, he served as a colonel of militia. People who met him noted that Johnson easily adapted himself to any company, equally at ease around an Indian fire as in the meeting rooms of the rich and powerful.

William Johnson (c.1715–74). Given the Mohawk name Warraghiyagey, Johnson explained that it meant 'A Man who undertakes great Things', indicating a political significance. It seems, however, that the name marked his 'great & toilsome Undertaking' in clearing the land after his arrival in the Mohawk Valley.

Brigadier-General Daniel Webb joined the British Army in March 1720, purchasing an ensign's commission. He later became a captain in Lord Ligonier's regiment of cavalry and as a major in that unit fought with distinction at Dettingen in 1743. Two years later, then as lieutenant-colonel of the regiment, he saw action at Fontenoy. In November 1755, he became colonel of the 48th Regiment of Foot, who had recently suffered heavily at Braddock's disaster on the Monongahela.

Webb was fortunate that he enjoyed the patronage of the Duke of Cambridge because others did not share his high opinion. When the Earl of Loudoun went out to America in 1756 as the new commander-in-chief of the army, Webb went too, appointed brigadier-general and third-in-command. Loudoun considered him 'timid, melancholic and diffident' and it seems clear that while in North America he displayed great caution at every turn, avoiding exposing himself to danger whenever possible.

Lieutenant-Colonel George Monro, 35th Regiment, was born around the year 1700 to Scottish parents in County Longford, Ireland. His father, also George, was a military man and as senior captain of the Cameronian Regiment commanded them at the battle of Dunkeld in 1689 when his colonel and major were both killed. The younger George followed his father's military footsteps and in 1718 became a lieutenant in Otway's Regiment (numbered the 35th Regiment in 1747). He spent his entire military career with the regiment, becoming a captain in 1727, major in 1747 and lieutenant-colonel in January 1750.

Marquis de Montcalm (1712–59). Montcalm saw much campaigning during the 1730s and 1740s. In 1746, at the battle of Piacenza during the War of the Austrian Succession, Montcalm suffered five wounds while leading his own regiment before the victorious Austrians took him prisoner.

After steady but unspectacular progress through the regimental hierarchy, and having spent almost 40 years quartered in Ireland, his military experience remained limited to the order and discipline of garrison life. Then, in 1756, came the order directing the 35th Regiment for active service in North America. Despite having no campaign experience, when Monro was thrust to centre stage he proved a courageous, resolute and honourable leader.

FRENCH COMMANDERS

Jean-Armand, Baron de Dieskau, born Ludwig-August von Dieskau in Saxony in 1701, began his military career at an early age and, in 1720, took service with France, becoming a protégé of the rising star, Maurice de Saxe, a fellow Saxon and later a Marshal of France. He served Saxe as an aide-de-camp (ADC) and tactfully, like his mentor, adopted a French version of his name. Dieskau accompanied Saxe on all his campaigns through the 1730s and 40s, including the great French victory at Fontenoy in 1745, and also undertook several diplomatic missions. At the end of the War of Austrian Succession in 1748 Dieskau's services received recognition with promotion to *Maréchal de camp* (major-general) and the office of governor of the military port of Brest.

As the situation in America deteriorated in the 1750s, France determined to despatch reinforcements and sent Dieskau with them as senior military commander in New France, but subordinate to the new governor-general, the Marquis de Vaudreuil. Dieskau landed at Québec in June 1755 to take up his command. Quick to appreciate the different nature of war in America he recognized the importance of Indians as irregular fighters, much as Saxe had done with partisans and other irregular troops in Europe.

Louis-Joseph, Marquis de Montcalm-Gozon de Saint-Véran was born in 1712 in the south of France to a noble family. He received an ensign's commission in the Régiment d'Hainaut aged just nine while continuing his studies. His father purchased his captain's commission in 1729 and he saw service in the Rhinelands in 1733–34 and throughout the War of the Austrian Succession, initially as an ADC and then as colonel of the Régiment d'Auxerrois. After the war Montcalm was made a *mestre-de-camp* and raised a cavalry regiment bearing his name. Then, in 1753, after petitioning the Minister of War, he received a pension for his '31 years' service, 11 campaigns and five wounds'.

In 1755, following Dieskau's capture at the battle of Lake George, the army looked to appoint a new military commander for New France. However, with the prospect of a major war in Europe in the offing no senior generals were interested in this backwater commission. Forced to look further down the list, the Minister of War settled on Montcalm. Montcalm later wrote it was 'a commission I had neither desired nor asked for'. But it came with a bonus. If killed in service the appointment guaranteed his wife a pension and also approved the appointment of his teenage son as colonel of the Régiment de Montcalm. With his family's future secured, Montcalm accepted the commission as *Maréchal de camp* and sailed for New France in April 1756. Contemporaries described him as short and a little portly, but active and possessing a sharp tongue.

OPPOSING ARMIES

BRITISH ARMY

British regulars

In 1754 Britain had three regular battalions in North America, one in Newfoundland and the other two in Nova Scotia. Two more regiments, the 44th and 48th, were dispatched following the appointment of Major-General Edward Braddock as commander-in-chief.

The 44th endured a disastrous introduction to warfare in North America at the battle on the Monongahela River in July 1755. Later, over the winter of 1756/57, they formed the garrison of Fort William Henry.

Prior to service in North America in 1756, the 35th Regiment had spent the previous 40 years in Ireland. After years of inactivity the regiment mustered less than 500 men, half the number required. The regiment recruited 80 men in Ireland and then took on a large number of impressed men and condemned prisoners from England, granted pardons if they agreed to serve in North America.

The original core of the 35th arrived in America in June 1756 and was joined at Albany in September by an additional 350 men – the sweepings of society – that brought the regiment's strength up to about 900 men. The officers had much work to do to form them into a battalion. Just over six months later six companies of the 35th Regiment relieved the 44th Regiment of garrison duty at Fort William Henry.

Raised for service in North America in 1756, the 60th (Royal American) Regiment uniquely mustered four battalions. Hopes of filling the ranks in America proved optimistic and it became necessary to draw recruits from overseas too. Many of the officers were foreign born. In New York there were also a handful of Independent Companies, each of about 50 men.

British infantry of the 35th Regiment of Foot, still known to some at the time as Otway's Regiment. Individual regiments were distinguished by the facing colours and the complex lace designs on their uniforms.

Provincial regiments

At the beginning of each year the Assemblies of the British colonies voted for the number of men they would raise for the coming campaign. The Assemblies then appointed colonels to form regiments and those colonels appointed their own regimental officers; personal relationships often outweighed military experience when making these choices.

Many volunteers had some militia experience prior to serving in a provincial regiment, but the familiarity between the officers, NCOs and men created an atmosphere in which discipline suffered. Volunteers were well paid for their services and recruits were not exclusively white; records show black – both free men and slaves – and Indian soldiers amongst their numbers. There was, however, no love lost between the regulars and the provincials, both parties having a low opinion of the other. The regulars, in an echo of a later war, particularly resented the provincials for being 'overpaid and undisciplined'.

While the provincial regiments lacked the training to match the British regulars, the manpower they provided was essential to fulfil the more prosaic duties required of an army in the field. But those who manned the barricades at the battle of Lake George generally fought well. Some men re-enlisted for subsequent campaigns centred on Fort William Henry but others, having grown disillusioned with military life, failed to enlist a second time. This meant provincial regiments always contained a high percentage of inexperienced men.

British-allied Indians

The Six Nations of the Iroquois confederacy (Mohawk, Oneida, Onondaga, Cayuga, Seneca and Tuscarora) had generally tried to remain neutral in previous wars between Britain and France. The Mohawk, however, the most easterly of the Iroquois nations, became pro-British in their outlook due to their proximity to the colony of New York, but remained unimpressed with British martial enterprise.

In 1755, William Johnson, charged with leading the New England army against Fort St Frédéric, used his close relationship with the Iroquois to try and draw them to side with the British. But he noted at the conclusion of discussions that he 'found all the Nations except the Mohawks extremely averse to taking any part with us'. By mid-August 1755 only 50 or 60 Iroquois had mustered, but later his friend Theyanoguin (called Hendrick by the British) brought in another 200 Iroquois warriors, the majority of them Mohawks. After the battle of Lake George, where they suffered significant casualties, these warriors returned home to conduct traditional ceremonies to mark their losses and only seven or eight were present in October. The following year, those Iroquois that attended Fort William Henry felt themselves badly treated, and in 1757 perhaps only 50 warriors regularly operated out of Fort William Henry and Fort Edward where they were often viewed with mistrust by the British.

Rangers

Ranger companies raised in New England first saw service in Nova Scotia in 1744. When the colonies began recruiting for their provincial regiments in 1755, Robert Rogers, a well-known New Hampshire man with experience operating in the forest, brought in 50 men. These joined Colonel Blanchard's

Britain made increasing use of rangers in a scouting role as the warriors of the Iroquois Confederacy demonstrated a reluctance to attach themselves to the Crown forces. Robert Rogers, the best-known ranger leader, was later immortalized in the 1940 Hollywood film *Northwest Passage*.

New Hampshire Regiment as a ranger company, with Rogers as their captain. The New Hampshire rangers moved up to Fort Edward and during the autumn of 1755, when the Mohawks withdrew, Johnson took advantage of Rogers' skills and sent him on a number of far-ranging patrols towards Lake Champlain.

Recognizing his achievements, William Shirley, governor of Massachusetts and the acting British commander after the death of Braddock, commissioned Rogers in March 1756 to form an independent company of rangers and also authorized the raising of other ranger companies. Their role was to fulfil the scouting duties previously performed by the Mohawks. Shirley insisted 'that none may be employed but good Officers, fit for the wood service, and to be depended upon, and I must entreat that none but picked Men, fit for the scouting service, may be enlisted'.

However, by 1757 these strict requirements were necessarily reduced and any man who was prepared to go out on scouting missions was generally accepted as a ranger. Ranger companies continued to serve throughout the war, but with varying degrees of success.

FRENCH ARMY

Regular troops

The first regular battalions to arrive in New France were the six that sailed with Baron Dieskau in May 1755. Having dropped two battalions at Louisbourg, the remaining four – La Reine, Languedoc, Béarn and Guyenne – landed at Québec in late June. Each battalion had an establishment of 525 men formed in 13 companies, including one of grenadiers. Fusilier companies had 40 men and the grenadiers 45. However, the battalions that provided men for the battle of Lake George – La Reine and Languedoc – suffered losses en route to Québec following the capture of a troop ship carrying four companies of each battalion. This reduced these two battalions down to nine companies each, a total of about 365 men. Two more battalions arrived in May 1756: Royal Roussillon and La Sarre. All battalions, other than the two at Louisbourg, participated in the Fort William Henry campaign.

In theory the company establishments saw an increase to 50 men in February 1757, but the trickle of reinforcements from France did not make up for the losses experienced by the battalions. All were the second battalions of their regiments.

It was common practice in the French Army to form elite *piquets* for specific tasks. These temporary companies of about 50 men were created by drawing together the best men from each of the companies.

Colonial troops, Compagnies franches de la Marine *(Independent companies of the Marine)*

In 1669 the administration and defence of France's overseas colonies became the responsibility of the *Ministère de la Marine* (Ministry of the Marine). To this end the ministry authorized the raising of colonial troops: the *Compagnies franches de la Marine*. These became the regular troops of New France and performed policing as well as military duties.

At the beginning of the 1750s there were 30 companies based in Canada with an optimal strength set at 50 men per company. This was raised to 65 men in March 1756, but companies rarely attained full strength. In March 1757 the number of companies in Canada was increased to 40.

While mainly recruiting the other ranks in France, the officers tended to be Canadian, born into military families. Because of this many had a good understanding of frontier warfare and were familiar with Indian languages. Inevitably, the recruits from France were a mixed bag; those unsuited to frontier life took up garrison duty in the region's towns and forts, while the younger, fitter men were distributed to the far-flung outposts that defended French interests and became actively engaged in raiding and scouting missions. These men, far from regular resupply, often adopted Indian clothing when their own needed replacing. At the end of their period of service soldiers were encouraged to settle in New France where their experience proved invaluable to the militia.

French regular infantry. The first regular battalions arrived in New France in 1755 as tensions with Britain increased. The uniform colour is described as grey-white, probably an un-dyed natural wool colour, with regimental variation demonstrated in turnbacks, waistcoats and buttons.

Milice *(militia)*

The *milice* formed a significant part of the forces deployed in the defence of New France. The authorization for the creation of the *milice* first came in 1669 at a time when the colony began to structure an organized form of defence. All male citizens aged between 16 and 60 were listed on a parish register, forming a company under an elected captain, and were liable to perform military and civic duties. The companies of *milice* reported for one day's training each month and neighbouring companies gathered for larger scale training once or twice a year. Serving in the *milice* was a civic duty and as such those called out for active service received no pay. Any extended absence, however, particularly at harvest time, could cause considerable problems for the colony's economy.

Because of the nature of life in New France many men were expert shots and experienced in bushcraft, making them ideally suited to fighting in the forests of North America where they readily adopted Indian tactics. Discipline, however, was suspect when exposed to a more European style of warfare. One senior French officer

described them thus: 'The Canadian is an independent, wicked, lying, braggart, well adapted for skirmishing, very brave behind a tree and very timid when not covered.' The *milice* provided their own guns but the government provided sustenance, equipment and clothing when on active service, the last item of which often differed little from that worn by their Indian allies.

French-allied Indians

The French, much more than the British, openly engaged with the indigenous American nations they encountered. As well as profitable contact with fur traders, the Indians also established important relationships with missionaries and officers of the *Compagnies franches*. Those nations drawn to the Jesuit missionaries, known in the language of the time as 'domesticated' Indians, settled at mission villages close to the St Lawrence River and regularly accompanied French raids. The best known of these settlements were the Abenaki mission at St Francis (Odanak) and that at Sault Saint Louis (Caughnawaga), where a section of the Mohawk Iroquois settled after being expelled from the Iroquois Confederacy. Other 'domesticated' nations included the Algonkin, Huron, Onondaga, Nipissing and Micmac. Away from the centres of French control, in the upper Great Lakes region (the 'Pays d'en Haut'), other nations were also pro-French in outlook. Of these the Ottawa and Ojibwa provided the most warriors.

On campaign Indians received provisions from the French but no pay. Money was not the motivator. Instead, they sought loot, scalps and prisoners for self-aggrandizement or exchange for goods with the French. Warriors losing a family member in battle could also forcibly adopt a prisoner to take his place. Some of the more brutal practices of their allies appalled the French, but their skill as scouts and woodland fighters was second to none. As one officer reflected, 'They are a necessary evil.'

As many as 1,800 French-allied Indians assembled for the 1757 campaign against Fort William Henry, the largest number mustered throughout the war. All anticipated collecting the rewards of their allegiance.

OPPOSING PLANS

BRITISH PLANS

Official news of the action in the Ohio Valley reached London on 5 September 1754 and by 24 September the government had appointed Major-General Edward Braddock as the new commander-in-chief in North America. The government formulated plans for Britain's response to the recent incidents and despatched two battalions of British regulars to North America (44th and 48th regiments) with artillery. In addition two new regiments were authorized for recruitment in America: the 50th (Shirley's) and 51st (Pepperell's).

The four-prong plan for 1755 was over-optimistic. It demonstrated little understanding of the problems presented by the terrain in North America and the difficulties involved in recruiting men, bringing the provincial troops to a state of efficiency and assembling the transport and supplies necessary for such a wide-ranging plan.

Braddock personally would lead the western attack. With the 44th and 48th regiments, and provincials drawn from Virginia, Maryland, North Carolina and an independent company from both New York and South Carolina, he was to capture Fort Duquesne and then push on to Fort Niagara.

Meanwhile, far away to the east, Lt. Col. Robert Monckton, at the head of a force of provincial soldiers from New England, was to sail from Boston, rendezvous with a detachment of regulars in Nova Scotia, and capture Fort Beauséjour. This fort, at the head of the Bay of Fundy, held an important position on a narrow isthmus that connected Nova Scotia with the main landmass of Canada.

In between these advances lay two more central attacks. William Shirley, governor of Massachusetts and named as Braddock's second-in-command in North America, led a force whose main strength lay in the newly created 50th and 51st regiments. He was to concentrate at Albany then push westwards along the Mohawk Valley, initially to Oswego at the eastern end of Lake Ontario, before pushing on and capturing Fort

Major-General Edward Braddock (1695–1755). Appointed commander-in-chief in North America in September 1754, Braddock commanded over a wide-ranging strategy, devised in London, which failed to appreciate the difficulties of campaigning in the largely trackless and heavily wooded American interior. The artist has shown him here in an American uniform of a later period.

The site of Fort Beauséjour. Work commenced on the fort in spring 1751 to oppose Fort Lawrence built by the British. These forts faced each other on the critically significant Chignecto Isthmus, the narrow point of land where Nova Scotia joined with the rest of America.

Niagara where Braddock would join him after taking Fort Duquesne. The final element of Britain's grand plan for 1755 rested with William Johnson. Braddock informed Johnson that he was to lead a force of provincial soldiers and Iroquois allies from Albany, north to Crown Point on Lake Champlain and capture Fort St Frédéric. Johnson, despite professing negligible military experience, accepted his role and began to organize his command.

FRENCH PLANS

While Britain was determined to launch a concerted attack on French territory, the French had no similar ambition at that time. A lack of manpower and the vast distances involved meant the main French intention in 1755 was to secure the Ohio Valley. Only when news reached Paris that the British were sending troops to North America did France respond with reinforcements of its own. The British campaign was already underway when the new French military and civil commanders arrived at Québec in June with four regular battalions. Considering their options, and taking into account their limited resources and the distances involved, they initially determined to focus on the Lake Ontario front. If the British established strong positions there they could threaten communications west of Montréal and the city itself.

Remains of Fort St Frédéric. This fort at Crown Point allowed the French to dominate movement on Lake Champlain and restrict British movement in the region. Completed in 1737–38, the fort featured an imposing stone-built four-storey tower unlike anything else in the region.

THE CAMPAIGN OF 1755

When news of the actions in the Ohio Valley reached France in the early autumn of 1754 it was too late for her to take direct action. Each winter the St Lawrence River froze in November and did not reopen again to shipping until April. In fact France did not despatch the Marquis de Vaudreuil, the new governor general of New France, and Baron de Dieskau, the military commander, until the beginning of May. With them sailed six battalions of regulars – about 3,000 men. The two men landed at Québec in late June with four battalions, having dropped off two others at the great fortified port of Louisbourg at the mouth of the St Lawrence. The news that greeted them was not good.

Fort Beauséjour had surrendered on 16 June and reports told of Braddock's slow advance on Fort Duquesne. They also learnt of the armies forming at Albany, destined for Oswego and Fort St Frédéric. However, the French were unaware of the excruciating delays incurred there as Shirley and Johnson struggled to equip and supply two expeditions in the same town and competed to recruit Indian allies. It led to lasting strained relations between the two men.

Considering their options, Vaudreuil and Dieskau realized that time and distance prevented them having an influence on Braddock's campaign against Fort Duquesne, instead Vaudreuil giving priority to defending the Lake Ontario front. Dieskau reacted quickly, organizing an army at Montréal of about 4,300 men for an attack on Oswego.

Further to the east, only on 17 July did the first 1,400 of Johnson's force of 3,000 men depart from Albany to march to about 50 miles to a remote point on the Hudson River known as the Great Carrying Place. There stood an old house owned by John Lydius, an Indian trader and smuggler. Widening and improving the track as they went, the journey took this advance party almost three weeks to complete. At the Great Carrying Place traders traditionally made a portage, carrying their belongings overland to the upper reaches of Lake Champlain. In a wild land lacking roads, with this one portage of about 15 miles, it was possible to travel by water all the way from British New York in the south to French Montréal in the north.

William Johnson arrived at the Great Carrying Place on 14 August, the last of his men struggling in three days later. In the meantime Major-General Phineas Lyman, commanding the 1st Connecticut Regiment, had begun to construct log magazines for the army's ammunition and supplies – which his men named Fort Lyman. These men had also commenced hewing a road through the forest towards Wood Creek, which fed into Lake Champlain.

'The warpath of nations', Montréal to Albany

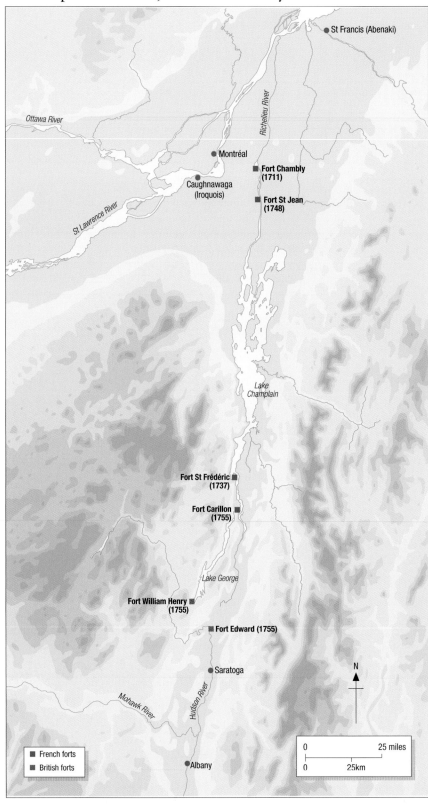

St Francis (Abenaki)

Ottawa River

Richelieu River

Montréal

Fort Chambly
(1711)

Caughnawaga
(Iroquois)

Fort St Jean
(1748)

St Lawrence River

Lake
Champlain

Fort St Frédéric
(1737)

Fort Carillon
(1755)

Lake George

Fort William Henry
(1755)

Fort Edward (1755)

N

Saratoga

Mohawk River

Hudson River

French forts
British forts

0   25 miles

0   25km

Albany

Johnson immediately called a halt to this work and, after sending scouts to Lac du St Sacrement, selected this route as being more practical for his artillery. At about the same time, however, Johnson received the disquieting intelligence that French troops newly arrived from Europe were moving towards Fort St Frédéric.

While Dieskau was at Montréal preparing for his campaign against Oswego, Vaudreuil received astounding information from Indian scouts on 12 August that Johnson appeared to be within two days' march of Fort St Frédéric. The information later proved wrong but, concerned by the vulnerability of the fort and acknowledging its importance to the defence of New France, Vaudreuil changed plans. He redirected Dieskau with the battalions of La Reine and Languedoc, along with troops drawn from the *Compagnies franches*, *milice* and Indians – about 3,000 in all – to reinforce that position and oppose any British advance. All had arrived at Fort St Frédéric by 20 August. Now the armies of Dieskau and Johnson lay just 50 miles apart.

JOHNSON PREPARES – DIESKAU STRIKES

On 26 August Johnson commenced his move towards Lac du St Sacrement, marching with 1,500 provincial soldiers and about 40 Mohawks, all he currently had with him. News of Braddock's defeat was now well known and had done nothing to inspire Iroquois confidence in the British. The news that the Mohawks' blood relatives, the Caughnawaga, had sided with the French also limited their enthusiasm for the coming campaign. But Johnson daily expected more to arrive. In the meantime his men cut a wagon track through the 15 miles of forest to the lake. He left behind his only regular army officer, Captain William Eyre, a military engineer, with orders to fortify Lyman's storehouses at the Great Carrying Place. Johnson arrived at the lake on the evening of 28 August and described the area as 'all thick wood, not a foot of land cleared'. He set his men to cutting down trees and opening up the land. Two days later about 200 Iroquois arrived at the lake led by the Mohawk sachem (tribal elder/leader) Theyanoguin, a long-term ally of Johnson. Within a day or two Johnson had audaciously renamed Lac du St Sacrement as Lake George, 'not only in honour to his Majesty but to ascertain his Dominion here'.

While Johnson's men continued to clear the land at the head of Lake George, Dieskau received intelligence of the fortification under way at the Great Carrying Place and reacted to the news that roads were extending towards Wood Creek and Lake George. On 2 September he moved his men to Carillon (known as Ticonderoga to the British), from where he could advance up either Lake George or Champlain, and awaited further intelligence before taking his next step.

Defeat on the Monongahela. After an exhausting six-week march through difficult terrain, Braddock's army was crushed in an ambush on 9 July 1755, just a few miles short of its goal, Fort Duquesne. Mortally wounded, Braddock died four days later.

An Iroquois word meaning the junction of two waterways, Ticonderoga forms a point where the La Chute River empties the waters of Lake George into Lake Champlain. Both Britain and France planned to establish a fortification here; France won the race and built Fort Carillon.

Back at the southern end of Lake George, on 3 September, Johnson ordered up the artillery and majority of the men left at Fort Lyman, leaving a garrison of about 500 men drawn from the New York and New Hampshire regiments. Johnson handed command to Colonel Joseph Blanchard, of the New Hampshire Regiment, with orders to complete the fortifications designed by Captain Eyre. The engineer officer, meanwhile, moved up to the lake to select a site for a fortification which Johnson's men began clearing. It was backbreaking work. As the camp continued to grow Johnson ordered forward the bateaux, the flat-bottomed boats needed to transport his army down the lake. Yet this work of road transportation proved a real source of frustration and delay. Many of the wagon drivers grew tired of the work and simply deserted. An exasperated Johnson considered them 'a parcel of rascals'.

On 4 September Dieskau received further important intelligence. An Abenaki scouting party brought in a prisoner taken near Fort Lyman. He revealed that the fortifications were not yet complete and that Johnson's army had marched for the lake leaving a garrison of only about 500 men behind. Dieskau decided to act fast and attack the fort with an elite strike force of 1,500 men. He selected the grenadiers of La Reine and Languedoc regiments and formed two *piquets* to strengthen them, each further bolstered by the addition of 12 men from the *Compagnies franches* – in total about 220 men – and backed them up with about 680 Canadians (600 *milice* and 80 men from the artillery, although he took no guns) and 600 Indians. Dieskau placed his Indians under the command of Jacques Legardeur de Saint-Pierre, a captain in the *Compagnies franches* and also an explorer and interpreter, while Louis Le Gardeur de Repentigny, an experienced *Compagnies franches* lieutenant, commanded the Canadian troops. Dieskau knew to rely on their experience and knowledge. He ordered his strike force into their boats at Carillon later that day and began the 30-mile paddle up Lake Champlain. By the end of the following day – 5 September – he had reached South Bay where he left his boats under guard and commenced his advance through the forest towards Fort Lyman (Johnson later renamed it Fort Edward).

Johnson busied himself in the camp at Lake George in the early days of September, still hoping to be able to move part of his force up to Ticonderoga if the French didn't occupy the area first. In the meantime his plan to build a 'good defensible fort', one 'which might stand against some artillery', met with overwhelming objections from his officers who voted at a Council of War for a simple stockaded fort capable of holding 100 men.

On 4 September Johnson sent out three Mohawks to scout towards Crown Point via Lake Champlain. The scouts initially headed towards South Bay but, on finding tracks of two or three men, they followed them. These tracks eventually disappeared, at which point the sound of gunfire then attracted the scouts, but that too revealed nothing. Only on the morning of 7 September, having moved backwards and forwards between South Bay and Wood Creek for three days, did they stumble on something significant. They discovered a trail, which they described as 'three large roads made by a great body of men', trampled, they ascertained, the previous day. Convinced an enemy force must be heading to attack Fort Lyman, the Mohawks headed back to Lake George. Johnson immediately sent a dispatch to Colonel Blanchard to advise him of this intelligence and then ordered out scouting parties around his encampment, doubled the guards and ensured his army lay on their arms that night. The man who volunteered to ride with the despatch to Fort Lyman was a wagon driver, Jacob Adams. About an hour later Johnson sent four men on foot to Fort Lyman with another message.

Dieskau had traversed about 9 miles of difficult terrain on 6 September – the trail found by the Mohawk scouts – and on the following day they covered almost another 18 miles, but things were not going to plan.

A CHANGE OF PLAN

One of Dieskau's scouts came in at about 2.00pm on 7 September and reported that the garrison at Fort Lyman were encamped outside the fort. Dieskau immediately decided to attack that night. But the commander already entertained doubts over the loyalty of his Caughnawaga Iroquois, and now they refused to attack the fortified position. Dieskau later claimed that when the Abenaki agreed to go with him and he told the Iroquois that he would attack without them, they changed their mind and demanded to lead the advance guard. Dieskau then claimed that the Iroquois misled him and took the wrong path. By the time he discovered this it was too late to organize the attack that night. He ended the day close to Johnson's road, about 3 miles north of Fort Lyman.

For Adams, Johnson's courier, this was unfortunate. As he rode up the road towards the fort one of Dieskau's warriors shot and killed him; the French captured a couple of deserters too. Dieskau now learnt that Johnson had about 3,000 men with him at the lake but had not entrenched his position. The dispatch also revealed that Johnson did not know the French strength. Dieskau called a council of war with his Indians and offered the choice of attacking Fort Lyman or the camp at Lake George in the morning. They chose Lake George.

A small reconstructed bateau (plural, bateaux) on display outside the Marinus Willett Center at Fort Stanwix. Bateaux are flat-bottomed boats of varying lengths, pointed at both ends, normally propelled by oars and extensively used by traders in 18th century North America for transporting goods. (Photo courtesy of Steve Vickers)

At around midnight the men carrying Johnson's second message returned to the camp at Lake George; they brought with them a wagon driver, a deserter. He reported that when about 4 miles from Fort Lyman he heard a shot fired and 'a man call upon heaven for mercy'. He believed the man was Joseph Adams. This news meant that the garrison of Fort Lyman remained unaware of the proximity of the French – and Johnson had no idea that French ambitions were now directed against him.

THE 'BLOODY MORNING SCOUT'

Johnson held an early morning council of war, which agreed to send out two separate forces, each of about 500 men. One would march to South Bay, to secure the boats that they presumed the French had left there, while the other marched to the aid of Fort Lyman. Johnson then informed Theyanoguin of his decision. According to Daniel Claus, an interpreter, Theyanoguin objected to the division of the force and threatened to withdraw the Iroquois if it went ahead. Some accounts say he picked up a number of sticks and snapped them one by one. Then, gathering a handful, he showed that together they would not break. Johnson reconsidered, cancelled the movement towards South Bay and detailed 1,000 men to march towards Fort Lyman; Theyanoguin and most of the 250 warriors in camp marched with them. Even so, the Mohawk leader remained unconvinced by the size of the force. He is reported as lamenting, 'If they are to fight they are too few; if they are to be killed they are too many.'

Johnson gave command to Col. Ephraim Williams, the 1,000 men formed from his own 3rd Massachusetts and the 2nd Connecticut commanded by its second-in-command, Lt. Col. Nathan Whiting. With the Iroquois leading and Theyanoguin on horseback, the first elements of the force moved off at around 8.00am. March discipline, however, was poor and the column quickly became separated, forcing Williams to halt his regiment near a large pond about 2 miles from camp to allow the Connecticut men to close up. After the pond the road ran through a narrow ravine between two mountains. When the march recommenced no scouts cleared the road ahead or pushed into the difficult terrain on either flank; Williams did not expect to meet any opposition until he neared Fort Lyman. The whole force was on the move again by about 9.30am.

Dieskau did have scouts out ahead as his men made slow progress towards the lake, the thick forest slowing the progress of his flanking columns. Sometime before 10.00am these scouts reported a British force on the road marching towards him. A deserter captured by the scouts at the same time revealed its strength. Dieskau immediately prepared an ambush. A brook meandered through the ravine and on the western side a steep bank ran along about 30ft above the road and which extended back across a shelf of land before climbing steeply. On the eastern flank the mountain rose steep and rocky except where it neared the southern exit of the ravine when the ground opened out. Dieskau's plan was simple. He later wrote, 'I ... ordered the Indians to throw themselves into the woods, to allow the enemy to pass, so as

Theyanoguin (c.1692–1755). The life of this Mohawk sachem (known to the British as Hendrick) has throughout the years become intertwined with another Mohawk leader, Tejonihokarawa, also called Hendrick by the British, who visited London in 1710. Recent research, however, indicates they were two different men.

Exactly what triggered the premature launching of the French ambush on Williams' command is unclear. However, once the first guns fired, the Abenaki, Caughnawaga Iroquois and *milice* concealed in the trees and undergrowth along the ravine poured a tremendous fire down onto the unsuspecting column. (Photo courtesy of Xander Green)

to attack them in the rear, whilst the Canadians took them in the flank, and I should wait for them in front with the regular troops.'

The Indians and Canadians were to remain hidden until the regulars opened fire. Those on the French left made good progress along the rocky shelf which extended for close to half a mile, but those on their right found themselves restricted by the extremely steep and rocky terrain and advanced no more than a quarter of a mile, the ambush forming the shape of a hook. With every man in place silence settled over the southern half of the ravine.

Some time after 10.00am Theyanoguin's leading warriors were between the unseen flanking forces, but not yet in range of the regulars, when a single shot broke the silence. The explanations for the shot are many and varied. Dieskau believed the Caughnawaga deliberately revealed their position on the British right to prevent the shedding of blood between them and the Mohawks, which caused the Abenaki on the British left to open fire prematurely. Others say Theyanoguin and one of the Caughnawaga leaders exchanged traditional challenges before one side or the other fired. Johnson later wrote that he believed a gun had gone off by accident. Whatever the truth, the ambush was triggered and a lethal fire poured down into the Iroquois and the shocked men from Massachusetts and Connecticut.

The Mohawks at the front recoiled from the fire and fought their way back down the ravine, but without Theyanoguin. A bullet killed the horse he was riding; having regained his feet he tried to get away, but, aged 63 and a little portly, he was no longer fleet of foot. He died, stabbed in the back. His assailants took a small circular piece of his scalp 'not larger than an English Crown'.

A 'prospective plan' of the 'Bloody Morning Scout' prepared by Samuel Blodget, a sutler in the camp at Lake George. The map clearly shows the 'hook' of the French ambush, Theyanoguin on horseback near the front with the Mohawks and the provincial soldiers under attack further back.

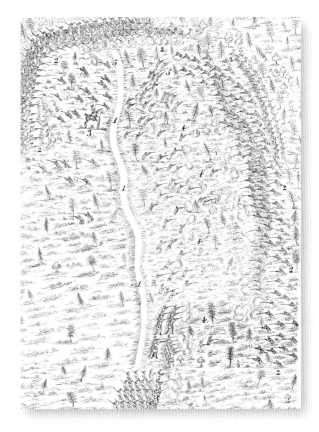

Monument to Colonel Ephraim Williams, 3rd Massachusetts Provincial Regiment. Erected in 1853 on top of the rock close to where Williams fell during the ambush, killed by a shot through the head. One of his men, John Morse, concealed the body in the undergrowth to prevent its discovery and mutilation.

Further back, Williams attempted to lead some of his men in an assault on the rocky shelf but the fire here was fierce and the attack failed. As he attempted to rally his men by a large rock, Williams fell dead, shot through the head. This fire proved devastating. Besides Williams, another seven officers of his regiment lay dead. Inevitably, with their officers falling all around them, these poorly disciplined men fell back as the French regulars rushed forward to join the attack. Some 40 of the Iroquois fell in the ambush too. Whiting, at the head of the 2nd Connecticut, made a stand for a while, giving cover to the retreating Massachusetts men, and they were joined by some of Williams' men and a number of Mohawks. They then fell back together, conducting a fighting retreat, making use of cover in the same way as their opponents.

When the first sounds of gunfire reached the camp at Lake George, Johnson stood the men to and began organizing his defences, which until now had received little attention. He had laid a line of logs around the perimeter of the camp, but this was not contiguous and in places these were no more than knee high. He now ordered wagons rolled forward to form improvised breastworks. Then, when it became clear the sound of gunfire was edging closer, he ordered Lt. Col. Edward Cole of Harris's Rhode Island Regiment to take his 300 men out to support Williams, who was clearly in trouble. This move delayed Dieskau, but one by one, and then in small groups, terrified survivors from the ambush streamed back, disheartening many in the camp. Only when Johnson and other officers drew their swords and threatened these men, declaring 'they would run them through', was order restored.

Johnson had a number of boats dragged into the defensive line too and

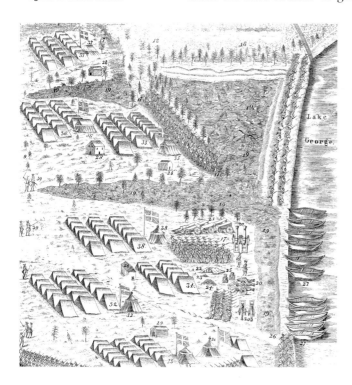

Another extract from Blodget's plan showing Johnson's camp at Lake George. Two gullies and low swampy ground dictated the camp's layout. Blodget explained that this 'occasioned the tents of several regiments to be placed in the form they are here represented, however irregular or inconvenient'.

26

positioned three artillery pieces to cover the road, placing another on high ground on the left of the camp. Lt. Col. Whiting's rearguard finally abandoned its regulated retreat about three quarters of a mile from the camp and fell back. The time was now about 11.30am; Whiting and Cole had delayed the French well, allowing Johnson time to improvise a defence.

THE BATTLE OF LAKE GEORGE

Dieskau halted about half a mile from the British camp to re-form his men, but his Indians again caused him concern; they were reluctant to continue. The man appointed to lead them, Le Gardeur de Saint-Pierre, lay dead, and it became apparent that the British had barricaded their position and cleared trees, opening up a killing field around the position. And there were artillery pieces too. The Indians had just fought a battle, they had lost casualties, they had killed and scalped. Traditionally it was the time to return home.

Although outnumbered, Dieskau remained determined to attack the encampment and made his intentions clear to the reluctant Caughnawaga, Abenaki and the *milice*. He would advance against the artillery with his 220 regulars and draw the enemy fire to allow the Canadians and Indians to rush the encampment. Lieutenant-Colonel Seth Pomeroy of the 3rd Massachusetts watched the men of La Reine and Languedoc form up with fixed bayonets about 150 yards from the entrenchment. He recalled that they, 'marched, as near as I can tell, about six deep, and nearly twenty rods [just over 100 yards] in length, in close order'.

Lieutenant Parfouru, commanding the Languedoc grenadiers, reported that initially a number of the provincial troops formed up in front of the barricades, shielding the defences from view. On Dieskau's order the

The initial French attack at the battle of Lake George. The Regulars fire volleys from the open while the Indians and *milice* fire from the trees. In the camp Johnson's men are lying down behind the barricades while three artillery pieces cover the road and one occupies the high ground on the British left.

grenadiers moved forward and the provincials dived for cover. Parfouru said his men approached 'to within 80 paces of the enemy … we ordered our troops to fire a general volley with the objective of immediately charging them with fixed bayonets. But we were really surprised to see only a defensive line and a few heads behind it; which made us stay on the defensive, by firing volleys.'

As the French regulars halted, the artillery, commanded by Captain Eyre, commenced firing and cut 'lanes, streets and alleys through their army'. The *milice* and Indians quickly dispersed into the trees on either side of the road. Out in the open the soldiers of La Reine and Languedoc began firing volleys by platoon for a short while, showing 'great resolution and good conduct' before joining the rest of the army seeking shelter in the trees. Thomas Williams, working at an exposed dressing station,

The battle of Lake George was the first battle many of the provincials had ever fought in. At times the officers needed to make great efforts to keep their men in the line. Many of the provincials had not received uniforms when they marched to the frontier in 1755.

recorded that 'the French bullets flew like hailstones about our ears … but … we received no hurt any more than the bark of the trees and chips flying in our faces.'

But he found the whole experience of battle confusing and disorientating; 'there appeared to be nothing' he continued in a letter to his wife, 'but thunder and lightning and perpetual pillars of smoke'.

Johnson had formed the Massachusetts regiments on the right, or west side, of his encampment with the Connecticut men on the left. Perhaps only 1,600 men were manning the barricades, behind logs, wagons and upturned boats. Another 500 were held back to guard the flanks of the encampment. With bullets now flying thicker than 'the hailstones from heaven', as Lt. Col. Seth Pomeroy described it, the provincial officers had to work hard to keep all of their men at their posts. About this time William Johnson received a bullet wound in his buttock and retired to his tent, passing command to Major-General Lyman of the 1st Connecticut Regiment. Some reports later emerged suggesting that Johnson remained in his tent for the rest of the battle, but others indicate he returned to the field after receiving medical attention. Perhaps the discrepancy had its roots in the rival colonial jealousies that existed in the army. Pomeroy recalled that both Johnson and Lyman 'behaved with steadiness and resolution' through the battle.

The fire of those attacking the British left gradually tailed off as the threat of the artillery proved too much for the skirmishing Indians and *milice*. Instead, they began to move towards the British right to join the attack there. As the French attack developed, Dieskau and his second-in-command, the chevalier de Montreuil, moved towards the *milice* lodged in the woods to the left of the regulars in order to encourage them forward. But as they passed just 70 paces from the British position, a bullet struck Montreuil in the arm.

A final detail from Blodget's plan showing the situation on the British right. Point 13 shows the two fallen trees which provided the Indians with significant cover while Point 16 indicates Colonel Moses Titcomb and Lieutenant Barron sheltering behind a tree while attempting to suppress the fire from those positions.

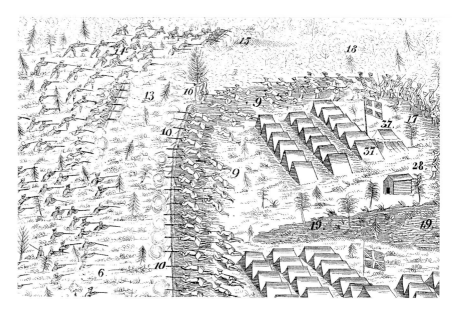

Battle of Lake George, 8 September 1755

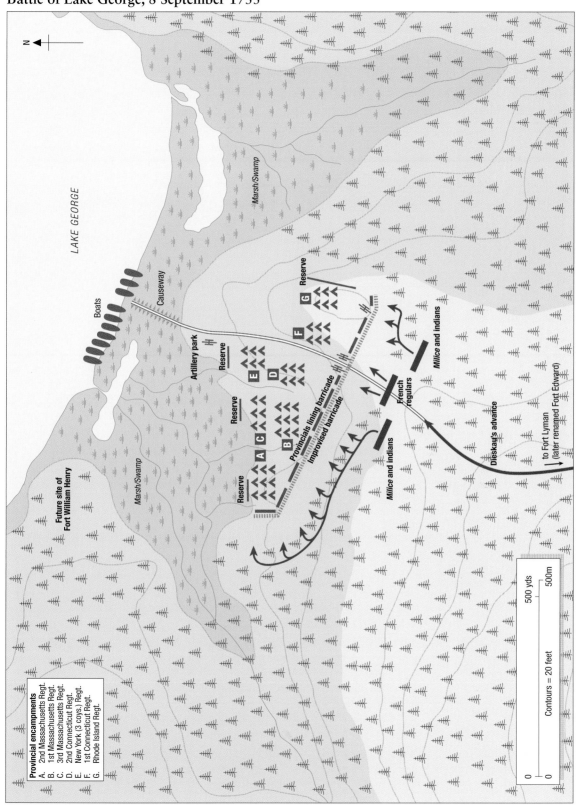

N

LAKE GEORGE

Marsh/Swamp

Boats

Causeway

Artillery park

Future site of
Fort William Henry

Marsh/Swamp

Reserve

Reserve

Reserve

Reserve

Reserve

A

C

B

E

D

F

G

Provincials lining barricade

Improvised barricade

Milice and indians

Milice and indians

French regulars

Dieskau's advance

to Fort Lyman
(later renamed Fort Edward)

Provincial encampments
A. 2nd Massachusetts Regt.
B. 1st Massachusetts Regt.
C. 3rd Massachusetts Regt.
D. 2nd Connecticut Regt.
E. New York (3 coys.) Regt.
F. 1st Connecticut Regt.
G. Rhode Island Regt.

0   500 yds

0   500m

Contours = 20 feet

Ignoring Johnson's orders, a number of the provincials crossed the barricade and entered the woods in search of loot. One of these men, seeing the incapacitated Dieskau leaning against a tree, fired at close range, the ball causing further serious injury to the French commander. (Photo courtesy of Leslea Barnes Photography)

Moments later another hit Dieskau in the leg. Montreuil tried to get his commander to move to a safer position but 'he insisted on staying on the same spot, though the place was not tenable'. As Montreuil tended to Dieskau's wound another musket ball smashed into Dieskau's right knee and passed through into his left thigh.

Out on the west side of the British position a number of Indians were sheltering behind 'a long large wind-fallen tree, upon a rising spot of ground, within [100 yards] of our breastwork'. From here Samuel Blodget, a sutler in the camp, reported they 'did us mischief'. He also noted a ridge of land about 80 yards from the British right that also had a fallen tree on it providing cover for 'some hundreds of the enemy (mostly Indians)' enabling them to keep up a steady fire, while only showing 'the tops of their heads … when they were about to fire'. In an attempt to suppress this fire Colonel Moses Titcomb, commander of the 2nd Massachusetts Regiment, with Lieutenant Barron, climbed over the breastwork and took up a position five or six yards beyond it behind a large tree. Both were shot and killed. While the engagement remained fierce on the British right, the action elsewhere had settled into a long-range exchange of musketry between those in the trees and those behind the barricades. The artillery there no longer had any targets in front of it.

Numbers of Indians then began to work their way into the swamp on the right of the British camp in an attempt to get in the rear. One of the artillerymen recalled that the 'General perceiving danger, ordered me to throw some shells, which accordingly I did'. Blodget noted the firing of two shells from the smaller of two mortars. The gunner added that they also opened on the swamp with a 32-pdr, 'which soon made them shift berths'.

The wounded Dieskau now sat with his back to a tree. Montreuil tried to have him removed from the field but he refused to go. Feeling badly let down by the Indians and *milice*, Dieskau pressed Montreuil to go to the regulars and urge them to attack the camp again. Reluctant to leave his commander, Montreuil objected, but as they spoke British confidence was increasing and a number of men crossed the barricade and edged closer. A musket ball smashed into Montreuil's cartridge box and flattened two of the rounds inside. He eventually departed but ordered two of Dieskau's servants to attend him and bring him off the battlefield. In the meantime the French regulars had moved further to their right to oppose numbers of the British who were emerging from the defences to try and cut off their retreat. A vigorous firefight developed in which the soldiers of La Reine and Languedoc, with Indian support, gained the upper hand, forcing the British to retire. When Montreuil reached them the regulars, having secured their retreat, had re-formed and were preparing to march away. Numbers of the *milice* and Indians had already left the battlefield, some returning to the site of the morning's encounter to collect loot and scalps. There would be no more attacks.

At Fort Lyman the night before, sentries had heard the shot that killed Johnson's messenger, Jacob Adams. In the morning Col. Blanchard sent out about 60 men of the New Hampshire Regiment under Nathaniel Folsom to 'scour the woods' and investigate. When they heard further firing, from the 'Bloody Morning Scout' encounter, they sent word back to Fort Lyman and were reinforced with another 60 New Hampshire men and 90 from the New York Regiment, under their captain, William McGinnis. As they approached the scene of the morning's action they found the French soldiers' packs and baggage, dropped before the ambush. Proceeding cautiously they discovered about 300 Canadians and Indians resting close to the pond where Williams had halted his men earlier that morning. Having already fought two battles that day, seen many of their comrades killed and been under intense fire for three or four hours, these men were now exhausted and demoralized. It was probably about 4.00pm when McGinnis commenced his attack, leading with 'the utmost calmness & resolution'. The French troops had no more stomach for the fight and a British report stated that 'our brave party fought nobly, put the enemy to flight, and made a considerable slaughter'. Folsom and McGinnis were both injured in the action; McGinnis died of his wounds two days later.

Back at the lake the French attack had petered out. Montreuil took command of the regulars but failed to get them to attack again, or even stand; instead they withdrew between 400 and 500 paces. He then heard Dieskau had refused to let his servants carry him to safety. Clearly it was too late now to return and forcibly remove him. Montreuil marched away unaware if his commander was dead or alive; he reflected that he was 'inconsolable for this loss'.

By about 5.00pm the battle appeared over, but Johnson, fearing the French were trying to draw his men out from behind the barricades, tried to restrain them. Ignoring his remonstrations, a number of men went out to search for loot. One of these men saw Dieskau lying alone against a tree. Although the French officer gestured to him not to fire he did so at a distance of not more than ten or 12 paces. The shot 'passed from one hip to the other, perforating the bladder'. Other soldiers came up, amongst them Lt. Col. Seth Pomeroy who had Dieskau taken to his tent. At about 6.00pm Pomeroy had the French commander transferred to Johnson's tent where the British commander was having his own wound dressed. Johnson ordered his doctors to attend to Dieskau first. Initially they thought his wounds were mortal but with good care he recovered. That he had the chance to recover he owed to Johnson. Furious at their losses in the battle and the death of Theyanoguin, a number of Mohawks demanded that Johnson hand over the French general to them. Johnson refused and eventually, with much diplomacy, placated his vengeful allies.

The battlefield monument in Lake George Battlefield Park, erected in 1897. The two towering figures represent Theyanoguin and William Johnson at the time of the battle in September 1755.

BATTLE OF LAKE GEORGE, 8 SEPTEMBER 1755 (PP. 32–33)

Following his successful ambush of a force of provincial soldiers and Indians at the 'Bloody Morning Scout', Baron Dieskau, the French commander, advanced on William Johnson's camp at Lake George. Fortunately for Johnson, a determined rearguard action gained him enough time to form a rudimentary defence at his exposed camp.

Dieskau halted to re-form his men prior to making his attack, but his Indian allies and Canadian *milice* showed a reluctance to take part once they saw the wide area cleared of trees **(1)**, the barricades and artillery in position. Dieskau was determined to launch the attack and made it clear he intended doing so. His plan was simple: to advance with the regulars and draw the enemy fire, thus freeing the Indians and *milice* to rush the camp.

The regulars of the Languedoc **(2)** and La Reine **(3)** regiments made their final dispositions about 150 yards from Johnson's camp before commencing a steady advance in line, three men deep, with bayonets flashing in the sunlight. Dieskau, sword in hand, urged them forward with the cry, '*marche, forçons.*' In front of the defences a number of the provincial soldiers stood in line. The French regulars halted about 80 yards from the camp to fire

a general volley, intending to follow up and carry the position with the bayonet, but when the smoke cleared the defenders had disappeared behind the defences.

As Johnson's artillery opened on the exposed French line, an irregular musketry from the provincials joined in. The Indians and Canadians had no intention of exposing themselves to this fire and took advantage of the trees on both sides of the regulars, firing from cover and refusing to advance **(4)**.

The French responded by making 'a regular fire by platoons' **(5)**. The French 'bullets flew like hail-stones' but their position remained very exposed. Frustrated, Dieskau moved off to the French left to encourage the Canadians and Indians forward, but, passing too close to the British defences, a bullet struck him and prevented him playing any further part in the battle. The exposed regulars of Languedoc and La Reine, lacking orders and with mounting casualties **(6)**, took advantage of what cover they could find and continued the exchange at long range.

Unable to make any impression on the British defences, and with their commander seriously wounded, the French eventually withdrew.

Montreuil had regained control of the La Reine and Languedoc regiments and organized them as a rearguard for the army as it retreated back through the woods to their boats. As they moved away the force from Fort Lyman appeared but Montreuil reported that they, 'seeing our good order did not undertake to follow us'. The battle was over.

Montreuil produced three casualty lists, which varied significantly. The last of these lists, prepared in October, gave 98 killed and 124 wounded. The regulars suffered losses of 78 killed and wounded or just over a third of their strength. Johnson recorded British losses at the three separate engagements that made up the battle of Lake George as 160 killed, 103 wounded and 67 missing, with perhaps over half of the casualties occurring in the morning's 'Bloody Morning Scout'.

Bloody Pond, possibly photographed 1890–1900. There is a belief that this pond has drained away and that the site now identified as Bloody Pond, although in the vicinity, is not the original. Its name arose from stories that some of the dead found close by were thrown into it, staining the waters red with their blood.

The day after the battle Johnson sent out burial parties and many of the names of those initially recorded as missing joined the list of killed. While his Indians busied themselves scalping the dead, or exercised 'their brutal dexterity' as one observer poetically described it, tradition has it that some of those bodies found in the vicinity of the pond, where Williams' command rested in the morning and McGinnis' detachment fought later, were thrown into it. To this day it bears the name 'Bloody Pond'.

BUILDING THE NEW FORT

William Shirley (1694–1771). Shirley served as governor of Massachusetts 1753–56 and operated as second-in-command of the army in North America under Braddock. Shirley became senior commander following the death of Braddock in July 1755 until superseded by Lord Loudoun. Shirley and William Johnson rarely saw eye-to-eye.

Although almost caught without any defences by the French attack, Johnson felt unable to immediately push his men to commence work on the planned fort by the lake's shore. The provincial soldiers were reluctant builders at the best of times. Now, directly after the trauma of battle, he felt 'it would be both unreasonable, and I fear, in vain, to set them at work upon the designed Fort'. He would wait for reinforcements to arrive from Fort Lyman before commencing work. In the meantime he continued to press for a more substantial fort than the stockade supported by his officers. They continued to oppose him.

Johnson's position did not improve when his Indian allies informed him they were returning home as was their custom after battle. They assured him they would return but they did not.

Pressure now mounted on Johnson from William Shirley. Shirley, confirmed as acting British commander-in-chief in America following the death of Braddock, urged him to make a move against Fort St Frédéric. But Johnson needed reinforcements, supplies and wagons to transport them, while many of his precious boats needed urgent repairs after their front line role in the recent battle. And all the time, work progressed only slowly on the fort.

Shirley's letters displayed increasing agitation at the delays and he also questioned the wisdom of building a fort at Lake George when Dieskau had proved the road to Fort Lyman lay open to advances from Lake Champlain. But Johnson and his engineer, Captain Eyre, remained convinced of the importance of having a secure base to fall back on if

The provincial soldiers showed a great reluctance to partake in the hard physical work involved in building Fort William Henry. The first stage involved cutting down trees from the surrounding woods – particularly pine and hemlock – before hauling them to the sawmill where they were trimmed and dressed. (Courtesy of Fort William Henry Museum)

needed when they advanced, and also the necessity of having one if the campaign failed to proceed at all.

Work on the fort, however, was not progressing well. The provincial soldiers, lacking enthusiasm for the project, only worked on it when forced and then with the greatest reluctance. News that the French had occupied Ticonderoga and commenced work on a fort there did nothing to encourage them to greater effort. Then, on 29 September, Johnson visited the fort to check on progress, expecting to see 500 men at work; instead he found not 'above a dozen … who were sitting down and no work going forward'. For Johnson it was the final straw and he angrily called another council of war. Finally he and Captain Eyre got their way. The provincial officers agreed to build 'a place of strength with magazines and stores houses and barracks … with all possible despatch'. Designed by Eyre, the new fort would hold a garrison of 500 men. Having recently renamed Fort Lyman as Fort Edward, in honour of a grandson of the king, he now named the new fort after another of the monarch's grandsons, William Henry.

The nature of the ground selected for the fort resulted in an asymmetrical design, with the eastern curtain wall shorter than that on the western side, with four corner bastions. The fort mainly used unseasoned pine in its construction, the logs hewn from the surrounding forest. All around the site, except on the north side where a steep slope descended for 20ft to the lake, a 30ft-wide ditch took shape, about 10ft deep, with a wooden palisade. The spoil from the ditch filled the void between the 30ft-wide double pine log walls. They rose about 10ft at this width then narrowed to a thickness of 12 or 18ft at various points around the structure, providing platforms for artillery to be mounted at embrasures and allowing men to fire over the walls. Inside the fort, brick-lined casements provided storage space under the log barrack blocks. But the sandy nature of the soil on which the fort stood raised concerns during the construction.

Once the logs were prepared at the sawmill, teams of oxen hauled them to the site of the fort. Work gangs using log tongs then positioned them according to the plan designed and marked out by Captain William Eyre. (Courtesy of Fort William Henry Museum)

Despite ongoing labour problems, the outer walls of Fort William Henry were completed and the flagstaff raised on 13 November, although much work remained to be done to complete the barracks and storehouses. By then any hopes of moving against Fort St Frédéric that year, or advancing to Ticonderoga, were at an end. As November drew to a close the last of the provincial soldiers departed for home, leaving just a garrison of about 400 men under Jonathan Bagley, the new colonel of the 3rd Massachusetts Regiment.

At the end of the year the wide-ranging British plans for 1755 had achieved little. They had successfully captured Fort Beauséjour, but elsewhere Braddock's advance on Fort Duquesne ended in disaster, William Shirley's attempt against Fort Niagara stalled at Oswego due to lack of supplies, while Johnson's advance on Fort St Frédéric remained anchored at the head of Lake George.

Elsewhere two lime kilns and a brick kiln were producing the materials needed to line the casemates dug under the fort's barracks. Some bricks were fired in the kiln, others sun dried. (Courtesy of Fort William Henry Museum)

FORT WILLIAM HENRY – THE WAITING GAME

1756, Oswego and a change of plan

At the start of 1756 William Shirley remained commander-in-chief of British forces for the time being. He planned two main thrusts for the coming campaign, the first, an attack against Fort St Frédéric and Fort Carillon, the new fortification at Ticonderoga. He appointed a popular Massachusetts officer, John Winslow, as major-general of the planned expedition, based on forts Edward and William Henry. The second thrust would be off to the west and directed against Fort Frontenac, which guarded the outlet from Lake Ontario into the St Lawrence River. Capturing Frontenac would cut the supply route to all France's western forts at a stroke. Shirley planned to launch this attack from the position at Oswego, where the garrison had barely survived a miserable winter, ravaged by scurvy and hunger. In March 1756, however, London announced a new commander in North America, John Campbell, the fourth earl of Loudoun. Paris also needed to appoint a new military commander to replace Baron Dieskau, now held by the British. They selected the Marquis de Montcalm to take up the sword, and only then did Britain and France officially declare war.

Montcalm moved quickly and arrived in Québec on 12 May 1756; Loudoun dawdled. His interim commander, Major-General Daniel Webb, arrived in America on 7 June. On 25 June Loudoun's second-in-command, Major-General James Abercromby, took over, but Loudoun did not arrive to take command until 23 July. Both Webb and Abercromby were happy to await Loudoun's arrival without taking any major decisions. Only towards the end of July did Winslow's leading provincial regiments begin to arrive at Fort William Henry in preparation for an advance down Lake George. At the same time Loudoun became embroiled in bickering and disagreements over

John Campbell, fourth Earl of Loudoun (1705–82). Appointed as commander-in-chief in North America in March 1756, Loudoun took over from Shirley who had held the position since the death of Major-General Braddock. Loudoun did not arrive in America to take personal command until July.

the status of provincial officers within the army. Meanwhile Montcalm was already marching for the British forts at Oswego.

Oswego proved a disaster for the British. The 50th and 51st regiments, reinforced by 150 New Jersey provincials, were wasting away in the complex of three badly placed and poorly finished forts when, on 11 August, the first of Montcalm's men invested Fort Ontario, the most easterly of the fortifications. Two days later, before the French artillery opened fire on the flimsy fort, the garrison withdrew across the river to the central fortification, Fort Old Oswego. On the following morning Montcalm commenced a bombardment of this central position, which, early on, resulted in the death of its commander, Lt. Col. James Mercer, 51st Regiment. About an hour later, under an increasing bombardment, the garrison raised the white flag.

After a less than resolute defence, Montcalm refused the garrison the honours of war, taking the whole force prisoner, but he promised them safe passage to Montréal. Initially elated by his easy victory, Montcalm was quickly brought face-to-face with the brutality of war as conducted by his Indian allies. Immediately after the surrender the Indians stormed into the forts determined to collect the rewards due them for their allegiance. According to one of the British prisoners the Indians found the garrison's rum supply and soon after 'became like so many hell hounds', butchering and scalping the wounded and other prisoners at Fort Old Oswego. Then they crossed the river and tried to attack the prisoners held in Fort Ontario. Only a stout and determined defence by the French guards prevented more atrocities. Montcalm was appalled and did what he could to secure the release of those taken by the Indians. It cost him, he reported, 'eight to ten thousand livres'.

In the meantime, after endless delays, Brigadier-General Webb had set out from Albany at the head of the 44th Regiment and a force of armed boatmen to reinforce Oswego. When he reached the recently rebuilt Fort Bull, previously destroyed during a French raid in March, he heard rumours that Oswego had fallen. Rather than scouting forward to investigate, Webb, fearing an encounter with a rampaging French army, ordered Fort Bull destroyed and trees cut down to block the river before he marched precipitously back down the Mohawk Valley. But there was no French army; Montcalm was on his way back to Montréal. When he heard of Webb's actions, Loudoun was unimpressed and, left feeling exposed by his subordinate's actions, felt obliged to cancel the planned attack on Fort St Frédéric. Loudoun had been in America for just a month; it had not been a great introduction.

Fort William Henry, summer 1756

With Winslow now acting on the defensive at Lake George, Loudoun sent three senior officers to report on the state of the fort as well as the camp positioned on flat ground south-west of it. It did not make good reading.

> At Fort William Henry, about 2,500 men, 500 of them sick ... they bury from five to eight daily, and officers in proportion. Extremely indolent and dirty, to a degree.
> The Fort stinks enough to cause infection, they have all their sick in it, their Camp nastier than anything I could conceive, their Necessary Houses, Kitchens, Graves and places for slaughtering cattle all mix through their Encampment, a great waste of Provisions, the men having just what they please.

The south-west bastion of the reconstructed Fort William Henry showing the log walls, embrasures and ditch with stakes. The stakes formed a continuous line at the original fort. The reconstructed fort opened to the public in 1955, 200 years after Johnson's men completed the original.

And there were concerns about the construction of the fort too.

> The Fort itself is not finished, one side being so low that the Interior is seen into (in reverse) from the rising ground on the South East side, also the East Bastion has the same defect from the grounds from the West, both of them considerably higher than the Fort, the Ditches being dug in loose sand crumbles away so that they are at present almost without form.

The report also highlighted damp casemates with rotting timbers, a damp powder magazine under the north-east bastion, a lack of beds in the barracks and water unfit for drinking in the well. And the list went on, bemoaning amongst other things, the poor condition of the artillery.

The report concluded by making a number of recommendations including raising the walls, re-digging the ditches and facing them with fascines to prevent them crumbling further and building a magazine for stores outside the fort against the north wall protected by a palisade. Although orders were given for a poorly constructed ravelin to be strengthened and improved, this was never done.

As winter approached the provincials' contracts expired and, released from duty, they marched home. Over the winter months of 1756/57 William Eyre commanded the garrison. The fort's designer became a major in the 44th Regiment in January 1756 and now held the post with about 400 men of his regiment supported by 100 rangers under Captain John Stark. Behind them, at Fort Edward, the garrison numbered about 500 of the 48th Regiment and four ranger companies. Those at Fort William Henry settled into their stark accommodation and generally remained on the defensive as the snows of winter descended.

Robert Rogers (1731–95). Growing up in New Hampshire, Rogers first served in the militia aged 15. In 1755, aged 24, he gathered 50 men and joined Blanchard's New Hampshire Regiment, forming a ranger company. The following year Shirley commissioned him to form an independent company of rangers that bore his name.

1757, a battle on snowshoes

When, in January, intelligence gleaned from a prisoner suggested the French intended attacking Fort William Henry in the spring, Major Robert Rogers led a force of rangers to Lake Champlain to observe French activity and, if possible, take prisoners who could provide more information. On 17 January Rogers led his command of 84 officers and men out of Fort William Henry and moved off across the ice of Lake George. Rogers pushed his men hard and the following day sent back 11 who 'had hurt themselves in the march'. On 19 January they left the ice and, donning snowshoes, set off across rugged country, by-passing Fort Carillon, until on 21 January they arrived at a position on Lake Champlain between Carillon and Fort St Frédéric. Almost immediately a sled appeared on the ice heading northwards. As his men moved to attack the lone sled others appeared, the attack triggered too early. These sleds turned to dash back to Fort Carillon but Rogers' men still managed to intercept three of them and took seven prisoners; the rest made it back to alert the garrison at the fort.

A quick interrogation of the prisoners revealed the garrison at Carillon numbered about 350 regulars, 200 *milice* and about 45 Indians, and that there were another 600 regulars at Fort St Frédéric. Rogers' small force was clearly in the midst of a hornet's nest and he immediately ordered his men to retrace their steps. At their previous camp they rekindled the fires to help dry their muskets, soaked in the drizzle that had been falling for some time. As soon as this was complete the rangers moved off, heading back to Fort William Henry. But the commander at Fort Carillon had reacted swiftly to the news of Rogers' ambush and now 180 of his men lay in wait to intercept the rangers.

The opening volley aimed at the rangers took them by surprise but did not have the effect the French had anticipated, the dampness causing many guns to misfire. Benefiting from their snowshoes, the leading rangers fell back on their rearguard and regrouped on high ground while the French floundered after them in the knee-deep snow. Reinforcements boosted the French later in the day and a fierce firefight continued until nightfall, but after dark Rogers led his men to safety and eventually reached Fort William Henry on the evening of 23 January. While both sides overestimated the damage they inflicted on the opposition, Rogers lists his own losses as 14 killed and six missing. He arrived back at the fort with 48 fit men and six, including himself, wounded. French reports state their own losses at 11 killed and 27 wounded, of whom three later died. But amongst the six missing men listed by Rogers – missing presumed dead – the French had captured three of them alive who gave up useful information to their captors as they prepared to launch an attack of their own, against Fort William Henry.

The battle on Snowshoes, 21 January 1757. Having first ambushed a French sled party, Rogers and his men then walked into an ambush themselves. Rogers received a slight head wound at the beginning of the skirmish but eventually managed to extricate most of his men under cover of darkness. (Courtesy of Gary Zaboly)

THE FIRST SIEGE OF FORT WILLIAM HENRY

RIGAUD'S ATTACK, MARCH 1757

Through the worst of the winter, French scouting parties regularly emerged from the relative comfort of Fort Carillon to keep a close watch on the activities at Fort William Henry. The information they gathered, confirmed by the prisoners taken at the skirmish on 21 January, showed that the British were building lots of boats, from sloops to great numbers of bateaux to transport stores. It suggested that the British were determined to control the lake in preparation for an attack on the French forts.

As early as 13 January Montcalm had proposed a raid on Fort William Henry to Vaudreuil, with the intention of 'burning, at least the outer parts of the fort'. He suggested a force of 800 men under a French officer. Vaudreuil rejected his proposal and devised a counter proposal. The two men never saw eye-to-eye. Montcalm had a very low opinion of the Canadian way of war and its use of Indian allies and disagreed violently with Vaudreuil's strategy. For his part Vaudreuil, Canadian born, had little faith in French officers after Dieskau's defeat at Lake George in 1755. He regularly praised his Canadian troops in despatches to Paris while criticizing the French regulars – considering them unsuitable for campaigning in North America – and also Montcalm's leadership.

Marquis de Vaudreuil (1698–1778). Born in Canada, Vaudreuil gained experience as governor of Trois-Rivières and later of Louisiana before his appointment as governor general of New France in 1755. Vaudreuil was the supreme authority in the colony but regularly clashed with Montcalm, who became military commander in 1756.

Vaudreuil made his plan to attack Fort William Henry a largely Canadian affair, giving command to his brother, François-Pierre de Rigaud de Vaudreuil (referred to as Rigaud). Rigaud had seen long service as an officer of the *Compagnies franches de la Marine* and since 1749 had served as governor of Trois-Rivières. The force Rigaud assembled was almost twice that recommended by Montcalm, leading to much grumbling by him and his aide, Louis Antoine de Bougainville, about the excessive costs of the expedition. According to Bougainville the force numbered about 300 men of the *Compagnies franches*, about 650 *milice*, 300 Indians and just 250 regular infantry. To counter the Canadian view that his men were not fit or strong enough to take part in a winter campaign, Montcalm selected the best men from the regulars to take part in the expedition. He put together a 50-man *piquet* of grenadiers, drawn from each of his four battalions, and four more

50-man *piquets*, formed of the best men from La Sarre, Royal Roussillon, Languedoc and Béarn regiments. Rigaud formed his Canadian troops into 16 mixed companies, each comprising 17 men from the *Compagnies franches*, 33 from the *milice* and completed with six officers and NCOs, giving a company strength of 56.

Commander: François-Pierre de Rigaud de Vaudreuil

Second-in-command: (Brevet) Lieutenant-Colonel Paul-Joseph Le Moyne de Longueil

Brigade Major: Capitaine Jean-Daniel Dumas

Commanding French Regular infantry: Capitaine François-Médard de Poulhariés
   (Royal Roussillon Regiment)

Piquet: Grenadiers (50 men)

Piquet: La Sarre Regiment (50 men)

Piquet: Royal Roussillon Regiment (50 men)

Piquet: Languedoc Regiment (50 men)

Piquet: Béarn Regiment (50 men)

Compagnies franches de la Marine: 300 officers and men

Canadian *milice*: 600 officers and men

Canadian volunteers: 50 officers and men

Indians: 300 (Abenaki and Caughnawaga)

Members of the recreated 44th Regiment of Foot in America. The 44th arrived in America in March 1755 and marched with Braddock to defeat on the Monongahela. Later, as the winter garrison of Fort William Henry, they defended it against a French attack in March 1757. (Photo courtesy of Ryan Gale)

The strike force assembled at Fort St Jean in February, over 100 miles north of Fort Carillon, and, having marched through sub-zero temperatures and days of snow followed by thaw, the well-equipped expedition finally reached Carillon on 9 March. They remained there for another six days due to bad weather and the fact that the rations for the attacking force were still being prepared. Rigaud collected 300 scaling ladders constructed for the expedition and was joined by Capitaine François-Marc-Antoine le Mercier, the colony's senior artillery and engineering officer, who prepared a large number of combustibles to be used against Fort William Henry. Finally, on 15 March, all was ready and, with the promise of calm weather, Rigaud's expedition began their advance to Fort William Henry. Two days later they encamped in the snow about 5 miles from their destination and the following morning sent forward captains Dumas, Poulhariés and le Mercier with an escort of 100 Indians and Canadians to reconnoitre the fort from a hill just over a mile from its walls. They reported back that only one small section of the fort appeared accessible by scaling ladder and, considering the activity at the fort, they felt the British were aware of their approach. Rigaud decided that if he could surprise the garrison he would attempt to take the fort, but if discovered he would concentrate on destroying the outworks and boats.

At about 11.00pm on the night of Friday 18 March, Dumas, two other officers and 12 grenadiers

moved as silently as they could over the ice towards the fort. But they observed that the sentries were well posted and alert so they waited for a while before trying again.

In the very early hours of Saturday 19 March, on a dark, moonless night, a cold but alert British sentry patrolling the ramparts of Fort William Henry heard an unexpected sound out on the frozen lake and sounded the alarm. Major Eyre described it as 'a noise of axes' – it was probably Dumas' men testing the strength of the ice – and then a light was seen. The garrison was alert. Dumas had seen enough and retired; Rigaud abandoned the plan to take the fort by surprise and switched his attention to destroying as much of the fort complex as he could.

Eyre had just 274 regulars of the 44th Regiment and 72 rangers fit for service, as well as 128 sick (mainly smallpox and scurvy). He called the rangers into the fort, posted sentries on the shore of the lake, manned the ramparts, loaded his artillery and waited.

Rigaud appeared before the walls of Fort William Henry in the early hours of 19 March 1757. Eyre ordered his men to line the ramparts. Of his garrison of 474, only 346 were fit for duty against Rigaud's 1,500 men, but the winter weather prevented him bringing any artillery.

THE ATTACK BEGINS

Some two hours later the French made their first move. Sentries manning the walls of the fort opened fire at a group of Indians and then another sentry, down on the shoreline, spotted movement on the ice and fired at a body of men approaching the sloops 'with faggots, fuse, & other combustibles to set them on fire'. Alerted to the danger, a 32-pdr cannon also fired and scattered the assailants who left behind 'a great number of scaling ladders, Tommihawks (sic), Scalping Knives, etc, etc'. The French made other attempts to set fire to the boats on the shore but much of their wood was damp and many of the combustibles failed to work; just a few of the bateaux were successfully burnt.

Fort William Henry, early 1757

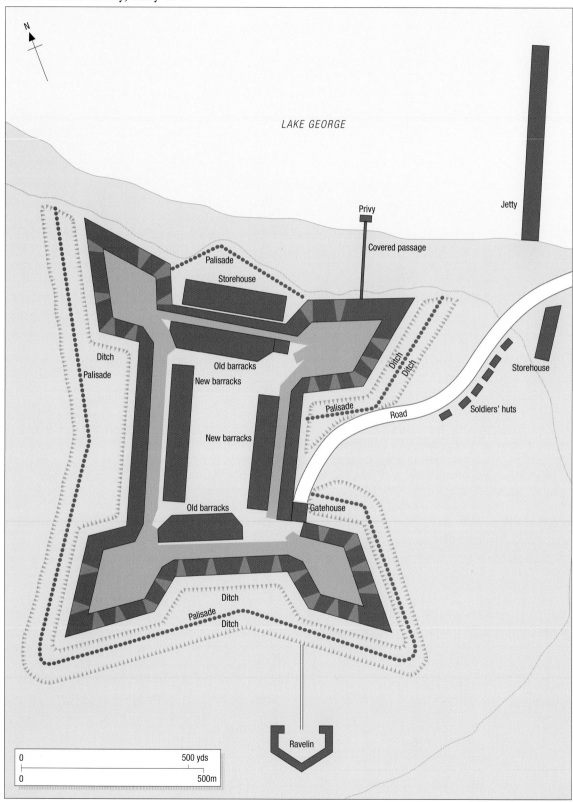

LAKE GEORGE

Privy

Covered passage

Jetty

Palisade

Storehouse

Ditch

Palisade

Old barracks

New barracks

Ditch

Ditch

Storehouse

Palisade

Road

Soldiers' huts

New barracks

Old barracks

Gatehouse

Ditch

Palisade

Ditch

Ravelin

0   500 yds

0   500m

At daybreak Rigaud's force appeared to withdraw and Eyre sent out a few men to try and discover the extent of the damage. However, a short while later the French reappeared in large numbers and seemed intent on surrounding the fort, keeping 'a heavy fire of Small Arms upon the Garrison' who replied with their artillery. Some French groups occupied the hill that Johnson defended during the battle of Lake George and one of the fort's garrison recorded in his journal that 'the major Saluted them with some Sower [sic] Grapes from a 32 Pounder which made them Hoop, and Yelp'. While this long-range skirmishing continued the *piquets* of the Royal Roussillon and Languedoc regiments were ordered to a position from where they could watch the road from Fort Edward for any sign of British reinforcements. The firing stopped some time between 8.00pm and 9.00pm, then, under cover of darkness, the French made a half-hearted attempt to storm the fort before stepping up their efforts to set fire to the boats and huts that surrounded it. This time they were more successful, setting fire to a great number of the bateaux. Then, in the early hours of 20 March, using the darkness to their advantage, the French succeeded in setting fire to one of the sloops, which burnt so brightly that it lit up the area around the fort for half a mile. But, according to one of the defenders, 'the Fire gave us an Opportunity to Discover where the Enemy Intended to Storm, or Scale the Fort, that our Cannon Scatter'd them from their Quarters, and killed some, which we could see by their Dragging the Dead away'.

Fortunately for the garrison the wind changed direction at that moment and blew the flames from the burning sloop away from the walls of the fort. At daybreak on 20 March the French withdrew once more.

To Eyre and the garrison of Fort William Henry, watching the French form up on the ice of the lake some distance away, they appeared very numerous and clearly showed the great number of scaling ladders they had with them. Then, later on the morning of 20 March, an officer approached the fort with an escort waving a red flag – the sign for a parley as the French national flag was white. Major Eyre sent out Lieutenant Drummond to meet the party. After taking delivery of a letter from Rigaud, Drummond tied a blindfold on the officer – Capt. le Mercier – and had him led into the fort for a meeting with Eyre.

Men from the *Compagnies franches de la Marine* warily approach the fort after nightfall. During the hours of darkness on 19/20 March the French made a half-hearted attack on the fort before turning their attention to burning the boats drawn up on the lake shore. (Photo courtesy of Geoff Ketcher)

Le Mercier invited Eyre to surrender the fort and offered the honours of war. And with memories of the atrocities committed after the capture of Oswego fresh in the minds of everyone, he claimed his men would offer protection 'of Mischief from the Savages', but warned that if the garrison resisted, despite the best efforts of the French, 'the Cruelties of the Savages cou'd not altogether be prevented'. Eyre rejected the proposal, later reporting, 'I desired him to make my compliments to his General, and tell him my fixt Resolution was, to defend His Majesty's Garrison to the last Extremity'. On that, le Mercier returned back across the ice. An official French account claimed this whole performance was a ruse 'to obtain information of a spot which appeared adapted to effect a landing in case our offensive operations were directed, next campaign, against this place'.

Major Eyre immediately ordered the strengthening of the fort with the addition of sandbags and the erection of swivel guns on the walls. He then toured the bastions and warned the men that the French would give no quarter. According to one they were 'not in the least Daunted nor Dismay'd but laughed at the Frenchs firing, and it is to be remarked here that a great many of the Men who lay sick for two or three weeks before came out on the bastions with their arms willing to partake the same fate with their brethren'.

And so the action continued. The French surrounded the fort and kept up a harassing fire throughout the day and on into the early part of the night. Then, regrouping under cover of darkness, they made concerted attempts to set fire to the sloops, bateaux, huts, storehouses and woodpiles that surrounded the fort. Eyre ordered his men to maintain silence so they could detect any moves of the French and then pour fire in that direction.

The intensity of the fires on the night of 20/21 March caused concern, but 'by proper care & vigilance' Eyre kept the danger from spreading to the fort. The French withdrew again at daybreak on 21 March but the Indians had already grabbed what bounty they could during the night's attacks. As an official report concluded, 'The pillage was considerable; the Indians were all night removing, to the camp, clothing of all sorts, guns, tents, a quantity of kettles, boxes, medicine chests, and barrels of various kinds of liquor, on which they got so drunk that they would have remained around the fort, wrapped in the sleep of drunkenness, had they not been removed before day.'

THE WEATHER TAKES A HAND

At about 9.00am or 10.00am on 21 March, heavy wet snow began to fall and an eerie silence settled all around. The French hoped to resume their attacks on the night of 21/22 March but the snow soaked everything and it was a hopeless task. Conditions were now very harsh for the besieging French and their supplies were running low. The terrible weather conditions on 21 March forced them to start burning the scaling ladders. It continued to snow heavily through the daylight hours of 22 March, preventing Rigaud from ordering the departure of his men.

During the day Lieutenant Wolff, a half-pay officer of the Bentheim Regiment serving as a volunteer with the regulars, offered to make a final attempt to burn the last of the four British sloops, the *Lord Loudoun*. It was the largest of the four vessels and intended to mount 16 guns; for now, though, it still lay on the stocks, its bowsprit just 15 paces from the fort's walls. Wolff received permission, selected 20 volunteers from the regulars to make the attempt and spent the day cutting and drying wood. Wolff's detachment moved towards the *Lord Loudoun* at about 7.00pm on 22 March but the defenders spotted them as they struggled to set it on fire. The men on the north-east bastion of the fort 'played so well with their small Arms that the French turn'd Tail'. Other attempts, against the palisaded storehouse lying close up against the north wall of the fort, met with a similar reception. If this storehouse had begun to burn then almost certainly the flames would have set the fort alight. Wolff's determined party made another attempt on the sloop between 10.00pm and 11.00pm, taking cover behind a large woodpile before rushing it. This time they evaded detection until the flames took hold and illuminated the scene. The defenders opened a withering fire as Wolff's men made a dash back to the woodpile. Just after midnight the sloop was burning uncontrollably. With the mission a success the raiders slipped away into the night. The garrison remained on the alert for the rest of the night but all was quiet, the silence only broken by the groans of 'One Miserable Fellow who was Mortally wounded'. In the morning Eyre sent out a patrol. They returned with three prisoners, one of whom died shortly after entering the fort. But it was clear that the French had gone.

TAKING STOCK

The casualties on both sides had been minimal. Eyre reported no deaths and just seven men wounded. Rigaud's force recorded the loss of two men killed and three wounded during Lt. Wolff's foray, with five men killed and six wounded in the other attacks – a total of seven killed and nine wounded.

Yet beyond the human casualties the raid met with great success. Without artillery the chances of taking the fort were always low but the collateral damage inflicted was immense. A French officer tallied up the following losses: 'Four brigantines [sloops] of 10 to 14 guns, two long-boats of 50 oars … over three hundred and fifty transport bateaux, a considerable quantity

A formidable battery of guns positioned in the Dauphin Bastion, Louisbourg. Louisbourg occupied a strategically significant position guarding the approaches to the St Lawrence River, a highway into the heart of New France. Loudoun planned to capture it in 1757 to open up the route to Québec.

THE FIRST FRENCH SIEGE OF FORT WILLIAM HENRY: NIGHT OF 22/23 MARCH 1757 (PP. 48–49)

The first French attempt to capture Fort William Henry took place in the winter of 1757. Led by Rigaud de Vaudreuil, the younger brother of the governor general of New France, the expedition marched up the frozen Lake George **(1)** without artillery due to the harsh weather conditions and hoped to take the fort by surprise. When Rigaud approached the fort in the early hours of 19 March he realised the garrison was alert and so turned his attention instead to the disruption of the fort complex.

The French limited their daytime activities to surrounding the fort and keeping up an irritating fire on the garrison, which the fort's commander, Major William Eyre, 44th Regiment, replied to with artillery fire. During the night, however, Rigaud's men made more determined efforts. On the night of 19/20 March they managed to set fire to a number of the garrison's precious bateaux drawn up on the shore and burnt one of the sloops, causing significant damage **(2)**.

The following night the French attacked again, successfully burning many of the huts and storehouses surrounding the fort,

as well as more of the bateaux. Heavy snow on the night 21/22 prevented further attacks, leaving the men, now cold, wet and hungry, to seek what shelter they could.

The French made one final attack, on the night of 22/23 March. An officer led 20 volunteers **(3)** intent on destroying the *Lord Loudoun*, the largest of the sloops, but which was still under construction. Alert sentries on the north-east bastion **(4)** discovered their first attempt and 'played so well with their small arms that the French turn'd tail.' A later attempt, just after midnight, met with success as the raiders managed to take shelter behind a large woodpile **(5)** without discovery before rushing the sloop. One of the garrison recalled that they 'could not see them until they had put the sloop on fire' **(6)** which, 'gave us such light that we could see … we fired among them very smartly **(7)**, and killed some, but as their custom is to take as good care of the dead, as of the living, we can't tell what number we killed.'

That was the last action of the first siege and later that night the French departed and struggled back to Fort Carillon.

of building timber, several campaign carriages, a saw-mill, the sheds and magazines which were inclosed by a stockaded fort, and finally all their supply of firewood.'

It does seem, however, that a handful of boats survived French attention. On 26 March Eyre wrote that a few 'Whaleboats, Scows, or Gundales & Bayboats escaped the Conflagration'. In addition two of the four burnt sloops appeared repairable.

But without doubt this was a serious setback. Any hopes the British had of mounting an attack on Fort Carillon that season had just, literally, gone up in smoke; months of hard work reduced to ashes in just a few days.

And yet the French had little chance to celebrate their success. Intense bright sunlight dazzled them on their exhausting march back across the melting snow and ice to Carillon, causing Montcalm to record the occurrence of 'a singular accident, namely, total loss of sight from the reflection of the sun on the ice. One-third of the detachment has returned blind. Canadians, Indians and our men to the number of fifteen score [300], had to be led by their comrades, but at the end of twice twenty-four hours, sight is restored with simple remedies.'

Having endured a long harsh winter and valiantly defended his post against attack, Major Eyre was looking forward to being relieved. In fact the 35th Regiment were already marching from Albany for that purpose when the French attacked. When Lt. Col. George Monro, at the head of his regiment, heard news of the attack on Fort William Henry, he left his baggage behind and made all haste to Fort Edward where he learnt that the French had retired. Lord Loudoun was happy to praise their efforts, writing, 'They all Marched without Tents, and lay in the Woods upon the Snow, making great Fires, and I do not find the Troops have suffered', and which they did with 'the greatest Cheerfulness'. On Sunday 27 March relief finally arrived at Fort William Henry when Monro led six companies of the 35th Regiment to the fort to take over garrison duty. Eyre was glad to bid farewell to the fort and the charred landscape that now surrounded it. As his men marched away they found some final grisly reminders of their recent encounter. Amongst their discoveries 'some of the French were found thrust into a hole made in the Ice, one man stuffed into the pile of Chord Wood, which they had set on fire, and an Indian, that the Enemy had covered with Snow and taken his Scalp off'. After Rigaud's departure, if Lt. Col. Monro anticipated a quiet posting on the southern shore of Lake George, he was very much mistaken.

STORM CLOUDS GATHER

The stage is set

As the snows of winter finally melted away, Lord Loudoun finalized his plans for the summer campaign of 1757. As he studied his maps the idea of a thrust straight at Québec emerged as the most telling strategy. And, frustrated in his dealings with the colonies, he intended making this critical blow an all Redcoat affair; he would instead use the Provincial regiments to defend the frontier, supporting regiments of British regulars detailed for that purpose. Back in London, however, the government favoured a staged attack, first capturing Louisbourg, the great French fortress on Île Royale (Cape Breton

Island), and then Québec. In the end, with the delays inherent in corresponding across the Atlantic, the final decision lay with Loudoun. Outside influences finally made the decision for him. A fleet from England ordered to protect the expedition arrived late, now Louisbourg was the only practical choice. Lord Loudoun gathered a large force of regular infantry at New York prior to shipping them to Halifax in Nova Scotia. From there he intended launching his attack on Louisbourg.

As part of Loudoun's plan he placed his third-in-command, Brigadier-General Daniel Webb, on the New York frontier. Webb commanded from Fort Edward with a mixed garrison of regulars, provincials and rangers. About 15 miles to the north-west lay Fort William Henry, the forward bastion in the region. Here Lt. Col. Monro commanded six companies of his own 35th Regiment, supported by two companies of rangers. As the weather improved on the frontier about 800 provincials – 551 men of the New Jersey Regiment with 231 New Hampshire men – moved up from Fort Edward to strengthen the garrison, along with 113 men from two New York independent companies. With the fort only able to accommodate about 500 men the rest occupied the former camp on flat ground to the south-west of the fort.

The success of Rigaud's raid in March confirmed French dominance in the region. The destruction of so many of the boats at Fort William Henry seriously limited British scouting, while the numerous French Indian allies moved relatively freely between Fort Carillon and the two British forts. Repair work began on the less damaged boats while construction of new ones commenced, but there were only a limited number of experienced boat builders willing to work in such an exposed location.

Intelligence and information

The British under Loudoun struggled to obtain regular intelligence of French intentions, hampered by their lack of Indian scouts. Loudoun maintained a low opinion of Indian loyalty, honesty and courage and did little to encourage their allegiance to the Crown.

The French, however, firmly valued the unique scouting skills of the Native American. Montcalm's ADC, Bougainville, while he showed great disdain for the methods and rituals of his allies, wrote appreciatively, 'here in the forests of America we can no more do without them than without cavalry on the plain'.

As spring moved into summer, intelligence arrived sporadically at Fort William Henry, gleaned from escaped prisoners, deserters and occasionally captured enemy soldiers. It told of French troops preparing another attack against the fort.

Then, around 20 June, Loudoun received intelligence that the French were withdrawing from the forts on Lake Champlain and congregating on Québec to defend the capital. The information was out of date but it corresponded with what Loudoun expected to hear. He informed Webb, 'You will have nothing to oppose You at Ticonderoga & Crown Point, but the Garrisons, and, I imagine, very few more for Scouting.' But by then Montcalm was already realigning his troops in preparation for an attack on Fort William Henry.

Loudoun advised Webb to verify the information and then, if confirmed, advised him to move quickly to establish a fortified post at the north end of Lake George. He airily dismissed the notion that there were not enough boats to facilitate this action. In contrast Webb felt vulnerable, lacking the strength

he believed necessary to defend what he considered a very exposed position. And still his scouts were unable to bring in detailed reports of French activity. While British scouts were failing to penetrate the French dominated woods, the French, however, were making successful raids towards forts William Henry and George, returning with prisoners and scalps. Vaudreuil was able to report confidently to Paris that he believed the British would remain on the defensive on the New York frontier and that Loudoun expected a strong fleet from Britain to sail with his expedition against Louisbourg. He concluded, 'From all these reports … it appears that the English are nowise active in following up their project of attack on Carillon and St Frédéric.'

By mid-July Vaudreuil could also boast knowledge of the British strengths at the two forts, as well as the number of artillery pieces at Fort William Henry, the number of boats available to the British on Lake George – and even that smallpox was evident at both forts. A few days later the British on the New York frontier became very aware of the danger they were in.

The Sabbath Day Point Massacre

At Fort William Henry, Lt. Col. Monro was desperate to gain clear information on French intentions against his post. On the morning of 22 July he ordered a reconnaissance in strength down Lake George. Led by Colonel John Parker, the force consisted of 300 of Parker's own men, the New Jersey Regiment (The New Jersey 'Blues'), and about 50 men from the New York Regiment. They rowed away in over 20 whaleboats. An advanced party of three boats set out two days earlier. The appearance of this advance party on the lake did not go unnoticed. On receipt of this news Ensign Charles-Michel Mouet de Langlade – son of a Canadian father and Ottawa mother – of the *Compagnies franches de la Marine*, went out to try and ambush them at the head of about 300 men, mainly Ottawa Indians with some *milice*.

The French dominated the 'intelligence war' between Lake Champlain and Lake George. Making great use of the unique skills of their Indian allies, the French remained generally well informed of events at the British forts; one officer maintained they were as essential as 'cavalry on the plain'. (Photo courtesy of Katy Turle-Smith)

Some of the islands, about 12 miles north of Fort William Henry, which form the Narrows of Lake George. Here, extending for about 2 miles, numerous islands clog the main channel of the lake and make it an ideal spot for ambush.

By the end of their first day on the lake Parker's main flotilla had safely negotiated their way through the numerous channels and islands of a difficult section of the lake known as the Narrows. Once clear and in open water again Parker ordered a halt for the night on a nearby island. But while Parker's men saw no sign of their enemy, a French scout boat spotted them and reported back. As soon as this news reached the camp at Fort Carillon, a Canadian officer, de Corbière, led another party of 450 men, nearly all Indians, and joined Langlade in planning an ambush. The forces concealed themselves close to Sabbath Day Point, a promontory on the west side of the lake.

In the pre-dawn darkness of 23 July the three lead British boats moved down the lake. As they disappeared around Sabbath Day Point, watching Indians launched their canoes and rapidly surrounded and captured them. A quick interrogation of the prisoners revealed that the main body would follow shortly. The Indians concealed themselves once more and waited, having manned the three captured boats to act as a decoy. As the British boats hauled their way beyond Sabbath Day Point they saw the three boats near the shore and pulled towards them. As they did so, Indians concealed along the bank opened fire. Parker's men turned about as the Indians dashed into the water with their canoes in pursuit. But others appeared from behind Parker's flotilla to close the trap. Only four boats managed to break through the cordon and get back to Fort William Henry. For the rest, their worst nightmares were about to become reality. Some provincials opened fire, but in their panic wasted their shots; the Indians were amongst them. Some leapt into the British boats hacking with their tomahawks; others capsized them, tipping the terrified soldiers into the cold waters of the lake. Some made for the shore, but found little respite there. Bougainville recorded that 'the Indians jumped into the water and speared them like fish... The English, terrified by the shooting, the sight, the cries, and agility of these monsters, surrendered almost without firing a shot.'

By the time the attackers' initial lust for blood had diminished, perhaps a hundred of Parker's men had been shot, hacked down, stabbed or drowned. Now they turned their attention to rounding up prisoners and perhaps another 150 were captured and led to the Indian camps at the north end of the lake. But that was not the end of the captives' nightmares. Father Pierre Roubaud, a Jesuit missionary to the Abenaki, recorded that later that day the jubilant Indians were drunk on rum discovered in the British boats. He found a group of Ottawa gathered around a fire. Having killed one of their prisoners they were cooking him in a pot and 'taking large spoonfuls of this detestable broth... The saddest thing was that they had placed near them about ten Englishmen, to be spectators of their infamous repast.'

Only about 100 of the expedition escaped, including Colonel Parker, and made it back to Fort William Henry on the afternoon of 24 July. There they regaled their horrified audience with shocking tales of the attack and their dramatic escape. Away to the north the French celebrated their crushing victory, one achieved at the negligible cost of just four men wounded.

At 10.00pm that evening Webb received reports of the ambush. Monro's decision to order the reconnaissance angered him; he complained to Loudoun that it went ahead 'without my knowing any thing of the matter till too late to prevent it'.

Nine days after the ambush at Sabbath Day Point, Father Roubaud passed the spot. He observed many bodies on the shore and in the woods. He described how, 'Some were cut into pieces, and nearly all were mutilated in the most frightful manner.' (*Massacre at Sabbath Day Point* courtesy of Mark Churms, www.markchurms.com)

However, it now seemed clear to Webb that an attack on Fort William Henry was imminent. A month earlier Webb learnt from a French prisoner that there were a large number of boats at Ticonderoga as well as many cannon intended to attack Fort William Henry. Four French deserters confirmed this information on 2 July, and then on 10 July a group of Mohawks arrived with a prisoner. He told of a large reinforcement of troops arriving at Ticonderoga and that Montcalm was 'hourly expected with the main body of the Army'. Combined with a fierce skirmish that occurred outside Fort Edward on the same day as the ambush of Parker on the lake, the evidence suggested that the French were about to make their move.

Webb inspects Fort William Henry

Webb had long maintained that the force under his command lacked the strength to fulfil its role on the frontier and he had informed Lord Loudoun of that. But now he realized he must see the situation at Fort William Henry for himself. Although Webb first arrived at Fort Edward a month earlier he had not yet visited this forward position. On the morning of 25 July, accompanied by Lt. Col. John Young, 2/60th Regt., Capt. Thomas Ord, Royal Artillery, and Lt. James Montresor, an Engineer officer, along with a strong escort, Webb marched to Fort William Henry. The garrison was still absorbing the horrific stories from the survivors of Col. Parker's reconnaissance when Webb arrived.

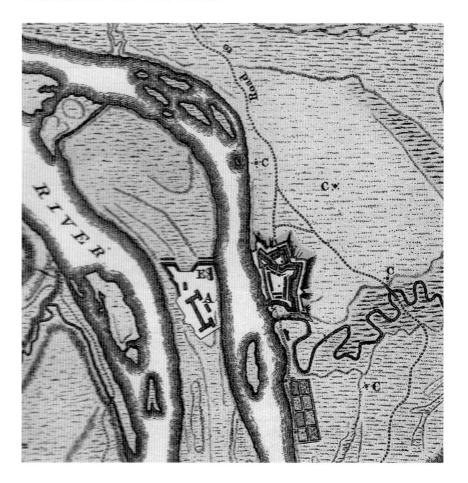

Built on a great bend in the Hudson River, Fort Lyman was renamed Fort Edward by William Johnson. From a few fortified storehouses it grew into a substantial fortification. The large midstream island became the base for Robert Rogers' rangers and is now home to the Rogers Island Visitor Center.

Webb ordered his accompanying officers to evaluate the position and they recommended abandoning the camp laid out to the south-west of the fort due to its proximity to the woods and distance from the fort. Further, they advised the construction of a retrenchment to contain a new camp on the high ground where William Johnson had anchored his position two years earlier. Montresor laid out a defensive line and work began on the construction of a log breastwork and ditch on 28 July. They also made a series of recommendations to prepare the fort for a siege. These included filling in the much-criticized ravelin, taking down the storehouse built against the north wall and the addition of firing steps around the ramparts and embrasures for muskets. In addition they recommended raising the east bastion one log higher and covering the roof of the magazine with sand to prevent fire and its air ducts with sandbags to prevent sparks reaching the powder. Fort William Henry became a hive of activity, but how much progress they made over the next few days is unclear.

On 27 July Webb held a council of war, which agreed that 2,000 men were required to defend the fort and new retrenchment. Webb also noted that after Parker's losses the fleet left to serve on the lake amounted to just five whaleboats. The two sloops that survived the March raid still needed extensive repairs and two galliots (flat-bottomed boats powered by sail and oar) under construction were not yet ready. Realistically there remained nothing with which to oppose a French advance up the lake.

Having got the garrison of Fort William Henry working with some urgency, on 28 July Webb ordered Capt. Israel Putnam and his rangers to take three of the remaining whaleboats to reconnoitre down the lake. At the Narrows Putnam saw three canoes at a distance. They turned away but Putnam did not take the bait. Mindful of Parker's recent experience, and believing he saw men in the trees on both shores of the lake, Putnam returned the same night and reported back to Webb.

After four days at Fort William Henry, Webb and his escort departed at noon on 29 July, arriving back at Fort Edward that evening. The following day he began sending out letters to order up urgently needed militia reinforcements. Firstly he required the militia of New York to assemble at Albany and asked William Johnson to also collect together as many Indians as he could and join him at Fort Edward. Then, activating an agreement put in place with the neighbouring provincial governors in case of emergency, he wrote urging the rapid assembly of their militias at Fort Edward. With the best will in the world, however, this would take time. Then, only on the morning of 2 August, Webb dispatched about 1,000 men from Fort Edward to reinforce Fort William Henry, as agreed at the council of war. Commanded by Lt. Col. Young, the reinforcements included 122 men of his own 2/60th along with Col. Joseph Frye's Massachusetts Regiment (812 men) and 57 men of the New York Regiment. They dragged with them six whaleboats to boost the diminished fleet and six cannon for the new retrenchment. The reinforcements struggled into camp at Lake George around sunset that evening, bringing the military garrison up to 2,351 men. The move left Webb with just 1,600 men fit for service at Fort Edward. Anxiously he awaited the arrival of the militia; if Fort William Henry and Fort Edward fell to the French then the road to Albany and the rest of New York lay wide open. As Webb pondered his predicament, Montcalm was already in motion.

FRENCH ARMY ORDER OF BATTLE, 29 JULY 1757

Maréchal de camp Marquis de Montcalm

Regular infantry	2,570
Colonial infantry	524
Milice	2,946
Artillery	188
Engineer officers	2
Indians	1,799
Total	8,029

Regular infantry brigades

La Reine Brigade

La Reine	369
Languedoc	322
Compagnies franches de la Marine	524
Total	1,215

La Sarre Brigade

La Sarre	451
Guyenne	492
Total	943

Royal Roussillon Brigade

Royal Roussillon	472
Béarn	464
Total	936

Milice brigades

St Ours	461
Courtemanche	473
Gaspé	424
Total	1,358

La Corne	411
Vassan	445
Repentigny	432
Villiers (volunteers)	300
Total	1,588

Artillery	188
Engineers (officers)	2

Indians 'domesticated'

Iroquois (from four groups)	363
Abenaki (from four groups)	245
Micmac (from two groups)	60
Nipissing	53
Huron (from two groups)	52
Algonkin (from two groups)	47
Total	820

Indians from 'Pays d'en Haut'

Ottawa (from seven groups)	337
Ojibwa (from five groups)	157
Mississauga (from three groups)	141
Menominee (from two groups)	129
Potawatomi (from two groups)	88
Winnebago	48
Sauk	33
Fox	20
Iowa	10
Miami	8
Delaware	5
Têtes-de-Boules	3
Total	979
Total Indians	1,799

Before Montcalm departed for Fort William Henry the Miami went home and these were followed by about 200 from the Mississauga and Ottawa leaving about 1,600 Indians for the campaign. Montcalm left behind a garrison of 100 soldiers at Fort Carillon, and another 200 to protect the portage between Lake Champlain and Lake George, as well as a number of the sick.

BRITISH GARRISON AT LAKE GEORGE, 2 AUGUST 1757

Lt. Col. George Monro, 35th Regiment (commanding)

35th Regiment	590
60th Regiment	122
New York Independent companies	113
Rangers	95
Royal Artillery	28
Engineers	2
Massachusetts Regiment	812
New Jersey Regiment	301
New Hampshire Regiment	230
New York Regiment	57
Total	2,351*

*This figure does not include the sailors and civilians who were present. One contemporary source states that there were about 150 sailors and carpenters present when the French first appeared.

From the above order of battle the following formed the garrison of the fort during the siege. (Detail from the Journal of Colonel Frye, Massachusetts Regiment)

Fort William Henry

Captain John Ormsby, 35th Regiment (commanding garrison)

35th Regiment	5 subalterns and 50 men
Massachusetts Regiment	2 captains, 6 subalterns and 300 men
New Hampshire Regiment	1 captain and 85 men
Total	450 officers and men

In addition there were a number of men from the Royal Artillery and sailors manning the guns, as well as carpenters for repair work.

THE SECOND SIEGE OF FORT WILLIAM HENRY

MONTCALM MAKES HIS MOVE

Fort William Henry had featured prominently in Vaudreuil's thoughts all winter. He wanted to follow up Rigaud's achievements in March and sweep away the British from the lake and from Fort Edward too. In May 1757 Montcalm had moved one of his regular battalions – La Reine – into Québec and positioned three others – Le Sarre, Guyenne and Languedoc – so they could march to the city in a few days, in case the British did launch an attack. Montcalm then moved the battalions of Béarn and Royal Roussillon to an advanced position at Fort Carillon. By June, however, intelligence reports showed clearly that the British were intent on a major seaborne attack on Louisbourg. Towards the end of the month, having analysed all the information, Vaudreuil gave his final approval for Montcalm to prepare for an attack on Fort William Henry.

The six regular battalions all arrived at Fort Carillon by mid-July. The men of the *Compagnies franches de la Marine*, formed by Montcalm into a single battalion on 21 July, joined them, as did a great number of *milice*, forming six brigades with a separate one of volunteers, and artillery crews to man his guns. But the most extraordinary part of the force under Montcalm's command was that formed by its Indian allies. Superb French diplomacy combined with victories in battle, particularly at the capture of Oswego in 1756, when reports told of 'everyone there swimming in brandy', drew warriors from far and wide. They came from 41 different groups belonging to 18 nations, some travelling up to 1,500 miles to join Montcalm's army.

By the end of July, Bougainville listed 1,800 Indians in the overflowing camps around Fort Carillon and right down to the foot of Lake George. He logged 820 as 'domesticated' and 979 from the '*Pays d'en Haut*'. They had not come for money, all sought the same thing: victory in battle, scalps, prisoners and booty. Each group was allocated a leader and an interpreter but it was an exasperating and, it seemed at times to the regimented minds of the European officers, impossible task to keep so many independent-minded warriors content, fed, supplied and under military control.

On 26 July, Montcalm announced that the army would proceed in two groups; one, travelling by land to Fort William Henry,

The Chevalier de Lévis (1719–87). Born to an impoverished noble family, Lévis joined the army while in his teens and made quick progress, earning a reputation as a brave and competent officer. He accepted his first staff post in 1746 and ten years later sailed to New France as Montcalm's second-in-command.

The French advance on Fort William Henry, 30 July–4 August 1757

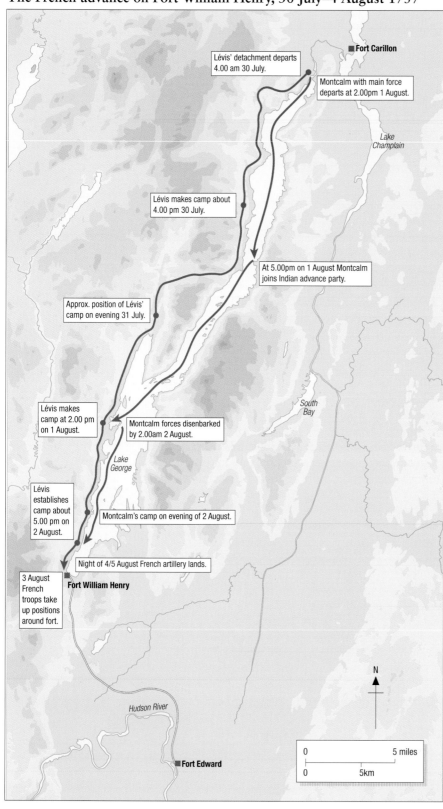

Lévis' detachment departs 4.00 am 30 July.

Fort Carillon

Montcalm with main force departs at 2.00pm 1 August.

Lake Champlain

Lévis makes camp about 4.00 pm 30 July.

At 5.00pm on 1 August Montcalm joins Indian advance party.

Approx. position of Lévis' camp on evening 31 July.

South Bay

Lévis makes camp at 2.00 pm on 1 August.

Montcalm forces disenbarked by 2.00am 2 August.

Lake George

Lévis establishes camp about 5.00 pm on 2 August.

Montcalm's camp on evening of 2 August.

Night of 4/5 August French artillery lands.

3 August French troops take up positions around fort.

Fort William Henry

N

0   5 miles
0   5km

Hudson River

Fort Edward

would leave in advance of the main party, which would make the passage up the lake by boat. The army Montcalm assembled numbered about 8,000 men.

François de Gaston, the Chevalier de Lévis, Montcalm's second-in-command, took command of the advanced detachment, formed of about 2,500 men. It comprised the grenadier companies from each of the six regular battalions (270 men), a *piquet* of regulars from each battalion (300 men), two *piquets* drawn from the *Compagnies*

franches (100 men), about 1,300 *milice* and volunteers, with 500 Indians. They commenced their difficult march at 4.00am on the morning of 30 July with instructions to await the main force at Ganaouské Bay (now the town of Bolton on Lake George). The excessive heat, mountains, rugged terrain and the need to carry all supplies and equipment on their backs made it an exhausting march. On 31 July the remaining Indians and about 300 *milice* – detached from those who went with Lévis – clambered into 150 bark canoes and with two bateaux set off to occupy a position about 9 miles or so up the lake on the eastern shore to await Montcalm. Then on 1 August Montcalm's main force finally boarded 245 bateaux, including 21 formed as two-bateaux pontoons to carry the artillery, and sailed at around 2.00pm. In all they carried 45 cannon, mortars and a howitzer, all of various calibres.

At about 5.00pm Montcalm's vast flotilla rendezvoused with the Indians and *milice* sent ahead the previous day and rested for a while. Then, delayed by a sudden storm, Montcalm's army finally, tentatively, approached Ganaouské Bay at about 2.00am in the early hours of 2 August. With relief they spotted the agreed signal, three fires burning. All was well and the army reunited.

Towards the end of the morning Lévis set out again with his detachment and selected a bay where Montcalm could make his next camp – probably that now called Diamond Point – about 4 ½ miles north of Fort William Henry. Lévis pushed his own detachment forward another couple of miles before establishing his camp at about 5.00pm, and then sent scouts out towards the fort. The Indians accompanying Montcalm hauled their canoes ashore a little ahead of the commander, close to a point that jutted out into the lake; beyond that point a direct line of sight ran to the fort.

After dark, alert Indian scouts watched as two unsuspecting British whaleboats, one of the regular patrols on the lake, rowed unawares towards Montcalm's encampment. The bleat of a sheep alerted the rowers that something was amiss; moments later the war whoop sounded and a swarm of warriors leapt into their canoes and shot forward in pursuit. The two British boats made for the far shore. Shots fired from one of the boats killed a Nipissing leader and wounded another, only making the

Mount Pelée, also known as Bald Mountain and now more commonly as Rogers' Rock or Slide from an incident linking it to Robert Rogers in 1758. It proved a testing obstacle on the first day of Lévis' march. With his usual brevity Lévis merely stated 'a bad ascent and descent'.

A typical whaleboat employed by the British on Lake George. This type of boat, pointed at both ends, proved popular as only the rower needed to reposition himself should a sudden reversal of direction be required. (Courtesy of Gary Zaboly)

pursuers more determined to intercept the British. They overtook one of the boats, killed four of the crew and took the other three captive. The other boat reached the shore where its seven-man crew took to the woods. Eerily silent musket flashes, followed seconds later by the sound of distant gunfire, alerted the garrison at the fort to an engagement out on the lake. This impression was finally confirmed when five breathless fugitives reached safety at the new camp; two others kept going and arrived at Fort Edward the following day. Back at the Indian camp screams pierced the otherwise silent night as relatives of the dead Nipissing leader tortured then killed their captives. At Fort William Henry the fugitives' stories confirmed the inevitable. The French were coming.

THE NOOSE TIGHTENS

Montcalm kept his men under arms all night then at daybreak ordered Lévis to lead his command forwards. Montcalm followed with the main body, while a large number of boats – carrying supplies and the artillery – nosed around the point and headed for the shore near where Lévis' men had spent the night. The British sentries were quick to report the appearance of the boats and the fort fired its 32-pdrs, the signal agreed with Webb to announce the appearance of the enemy. Some of the French guns, way out of range, replied from their precarious platforms to intimidate the garrison. Lt. Col. Monro penned a brief note to Webb and dispatched it immediately. He advised that 'the enemy are in sight upon the lake, and we know that they have cannon'. Webb received it at about 1.00pm. His worst fears had just been realized. He immediately sent a dispatch to Albany urging the deputy assistant quartermaster general there to send up the garrison as well as any militia ready to march, then he requested Sir William Johnson's immediate presence with what force he could gather.

This photo shows the south shore of Lake George as it appeared at the beginning of the 20th century before major development began. The growth of darker trees just to the right of centre marks the site of Fort William Henry.

When the French appeared on the lake, Monro sent Capt. John Ormsby, 35th Regiment, to take command of the fort at the head of a fresh detachment of two companies of the Massachusetts Regiment along with some officers and men of the 35th to give the garrison a regular infantry backbone. The men started rounding up the grazing livestock and burning outlying huts and undergrowth on the western side of the fort to prevent them providing cover for the enemy. At the same time those at the new retrenchment continued strengthening the position as best they could.

Around 9.00am white-coated French regulars appeared and began moving around to the south-west of the fort at a distance of about 1,000 yards, whereupon Lt. Thomas Collins, Royal Artillery, commanding the guns in the fort, opened fire. Earlier Lt. Col. Monro sent out a detachment of about 100 Massachusetts provincials and rangers from the camp, commanded by Capt. Richard Saltonstall, to occupy a position on the road to Fort Edward. Lévis' Indians were already swarming through the trees intent on occupying the road too. Some of the livestock that had been rounded up earlier had broken free from their enclosure when the firing started at the fort. The Indians began shooting them and also captured 25 cattle before engaging in a fierce firefight with Saltonstall's men. Eventually overwhelmed, the detachment fell back on the camp having lost an officer and 18 men killed as well as several others wounded. The Indians kept up a constant fire on the retrenchment to which the defenders replied vigorously, but only when a 12-pdr in the camp

opened up with grapeshot did the Indians draw back. The noise of all this firing was very apparent at Fort Edward, and Webb dispatched two small ranger scouting parties to gather intelligence. Monro wrote another brief note at about 9.00am; he was beginning to feel exposed. He informed Webb, 'We have a few men wounded by their random shot, but their body has not yet appeared. I believe you will think it proper to send a reinforcement as soon as possible. I can tell you nothing at present.'

Montcalm now joined Lévis to evaluate the position. He had a loose cordon around the fort and retrenchment but recognized it would prove costly to launch an assault against the camp and would also be difficult to keep a large attacking force supplied while the fort remained secure in their rear. The decision was made; Montcalm ordered the army to start forming camps for a siege of Fort William Henry. Lévis, with the Indians and *milice*, would remain occupying the advanced position from where he could harass the garrisons of both the fort and camp, while also watching the road from Fort Edward.

In the early afternoon, having made his decision, Montcalm sent an aide, Capitaine Fontbrune, to deliver a summons to surrender. The letter handed to Monro advised him that the French had invested his position 'with a numerous Army and superior Artillery, and all the savages from the High Country, the Cruelty of which, a Detachment of your Garrison have lately too much experienced'.

Using the threat of Indian brutality, Montcalm naively claimed he could restrain his allies if the garrison surrendered immediately, but that would no longer be in his power if Monro insisted on defending his position. And, he added, any resistance would be a pointless waste of life as it could only delay him by a few days at most. Monro, being conversant with the etiquette of siege warfare, defiantly rejected Montcalm's proposal and trusted to Webb to forward reinforcements.

At about 6.00pm, Monro prepared another dispatch for Webb and, once the day gave way to night, he managed to send it off along with the earlier note written at 9.00am. He advised Webb that he had rejected the summons to surrender and informed him that the French had not yet constructed their batteries but that the garrison had been under fire all day. In closing, Monro stressed again the need for support, adding, 'I make no doubt that you will

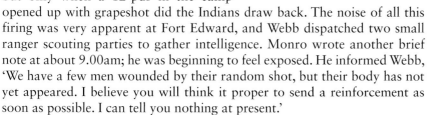

Early on 3 August a body of rangers and provincials went out to occupy a position on the road to Fort Edward. There they engaged in a fierce firefight with the large numbers of Indians swarming through the woods, but were eventually driven back on camp. (Photo courtesy of Xander Green)

soon send us a reinforcement.' Then, as a last thought, he added, 'The men all seem to be in good spirits.' As darkness settled over the lake, all firing gradually died out, just the occasional shot breaking the silence of the night.

That evening one of the ranger scouting groups dispatched by Webb stealthily approached the loosely cordoned British position and spied a lone Canadian, an officer in the *milice*. As he cut some meat from one of the cows shot earlier in the day, they seized him and silently melted back into the dark of the forest.

THE SIEGE – DAY 1 – THE GARRISON STANDS ALONE

At daybreak on 4 August, Montcalm began to re-form his army. All the regulars rejoined their parent units, including the detached grenadier and infantry *piquets* that had marched with Lévis. Montcalm left him four of the *milice* brigades and de Villier's volunteers (2,060 men) and the Indians (about 1,600 warriors) to control the area to the south of the fort and camp.

While the Indians edged towards the British positions and opened a regular fire on any target they could locate, Montcalm and Colonel François-Charles de Bourlamaque, along with the other artillery and engineer officers, studied the fort. They drew up their siege plans and ordered the construction of a road from the cove where the artillery would land to the head of the trench. Work began at 1.00pm. All this activity did not go unnoticed and as it intensified so the British guns in the fort began to fire 'a great deal of shot and shell' hoping to disrupt the work. Under this fire the French battled on against the fallen trees and stumps that littered the ground, but gained a little relief during this long-range bombardment when one of the fort's mortars burst. There were no serious injuries but it was a sign of things to come. Many of the fort's guns were made of iron, including all the large calibre ones. Iron guns were more prone than bronze to metal fatigue, which could cause them to burst without warning. The fort mounted 17 cannon, three mortars, a howitzer and 13 swivel guns. Another six cannon and four swivel guns protected the camp.

There was action around the camp too when a large number of *milice* and Indians attempted to cut the garrison's route to their water supply. Monro ordered out about 100 Massachusetts provincials, commanded by Capt. Ralph Waldo, who occupied some rising ground and forced the attackers

Situation at Fort William Henry, late morning 4 August 1757

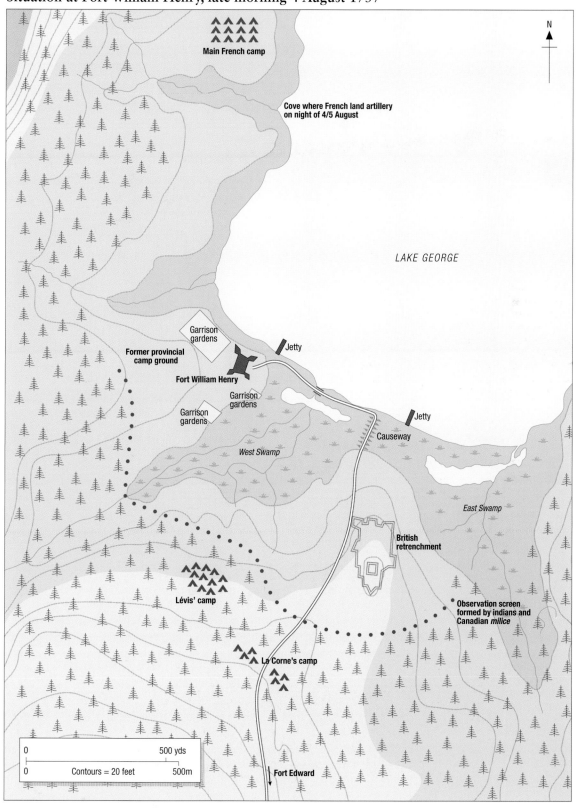

Main French camp

Cove where French land artillery
on night of 4/5 August

N

LAKE GEORGE

Garrison
gardens

Jetty

**Former provincial
camp ground**

Fort William Henry

Garrison
gardens

Jetty

Garrison
gardens

West Swamp

Causeway

East Swamp

**British
retrenchment**

Lévis' camp

**Observation screen
formed by indians and
Canadian *milice***

Le Corne's camp

0   500 yds

0   500m
Contours = 20 feet

↓ **Fort Edward**

Fort Edward August 4th 12 o'clock at Noon

Sir

I am directed by General Webb to acknowledge the receipt of three of your Letters, two bearing Date about nine yesterday morning, and one about six in the Evening by two Rangers, which are the only men that have got in here, except two yesterday morning with your first acquainting him of the Enemy being in sight. He has order'd me to acquaint you he does not think it prudent (as you know his strength at this place) to attempt a Junction or to assist you till reinforc'd by the Militia of the Provinces, for the immediate march of which repeated Expresses have been sent. One of our Scouts brought in a Canadian Prisr. last night from the investing Party which is very large, and have possess'd all the Grounds five miles on this side of Fort Wm Henry. The number of the Enemy is very considerable, the Prisr. says eleven thousand and have a large Train of artillery with Mortars and were to open their Batteries this day. The General thought proper to give you this intelligence, that in case he should be so unfortunate from the delays of the Militia not to [have it in his power to] give you timely Assistance, you might be able to make the best terms were left in your power. The Bearer is a Serjt of the Connecticut Forces, and if is happy enough to get in will bring advices from you. we keep continual Scouts going to endeavor to get in, or bring intelligence from you.

I am Sir, with the heartiest and most anxious wishes for your Welfare
your most Obedient
Humble Servant
G. Bartman
Aid de Camp.

Lt. Col: Monro or Officer
Commanding at Fort Wm Henry.

The actual letter written by Webb's ADC to George Monro, advising him to seek terms if the militia did not appear. The letter, folded as small as possible, was hidden 'in the vest' of a ranger sergeant entrusted to carry the despatch. The dark stain on the left edge is his blood. (Courtesy of The Huntington Library, San Marino, California)

back; however, they soon found themselves outflanked. Monro reinforced them but the position became untenable and all fell back, carrying the mortally wounded Waldo with them. The attackers followed up aggressively and only the close attention of the camp's artillery forced them to disperse.

At Fort Edward, the sound of firing coming from the lake seemed to tail off in the afternoon, but Webb now found himself in a difficult situation. In the early hours the ranger scouting party had returned from Lake George with their Canadian prisoner. He provided the first detailed information of events taking place at the lake. The prisoner, Jacques Vaudry de la Chesnaye, revealed to Webb an inflated estimate of French strength, stating that Montcalm had between 11,000 and 12,000 men. At that moment Webb had 2,351 men under arms at the lake along with maybe 150 sailors and carpenters, and just 1,600 at Fort Edward. The first of the reinforcements he had called forward were due to start arriving later that day, but it would be a trickle, not a flood, of men. This information coincided with the receipt of Monro's letters written at 9.00am and 6.00pm the previous day. Webb, a cautious officer at the best of times, was in no position to abandon Fort Edward and risk all by marching with his 1,600 men to reinforce Monro. He now believed the French had a vastly superior force at the lake and even had he known the truth, that the French in fact now numbered less than 8,000 men, he would not have left Fort Edward undefended and the road to Albany open to join battle against a force twice his size. And if he had, and his 1,600 men had been surprised by Lévis' covering force of over 3,000 *milice* and Indians, then outcomes similar to that suffered in 1755 by Braddock on the Monongahela or by the colonial detachment at the 'Bloody Morning Scout', can easily be imagined. At noon on 4 August Webb prepared his now infamous despatch to Monro. Written by his ADC, Captain George Bartman, it provided bleak reading: 'He [Webb] has ordered me to acquaint you he does not think it prudent as you know his strength at this place, to attempt a junction or to join you till reinforced by the militia of the colonies, for the march of which repeated requests have been sent.'

The letter went on to acquaint Monro of the intelligence he had from the prisoner concerning the strength of the besieging force. Bartman then concluded by offering Monro some advice: 'The General thought proper to give you this intelligence, that in case he should be so unfortunate from delay of the militia not to have it in his power to give you timely assistance you might be able to make the best terms as were left in your power.'

He folded the letter as small as possible and had it sewn into the jacket of a sergeant of the rangers, who then set off with two comrades to try and get through to Fort William Henry. The letter did eventually reach Monro three days later, but not in the way Webb had intended.

Unaware of this letter, Monro wrote at 6.00pm that he had not yet seen the French regulars and presumed they were working on the batteries. Then, he added, 'as we are very certain that part of the enemy have got between you and us upon the high road, would therefore be glad (if it meets with your approbation) the whole army was marched'.

THE SIEGE – DAY 2 – MONTCALM'S TRUMP CARD

Some 450 French troops worked all through the night of 4/5 August. They pushed a trench forwards and commenced work on the first battery while opening a parallel towards a second. They also landed 12 artillery pieces and some mortars. At first light on 5 August a fresh working party of 200 men took over.

The artillery in the fort kept up a regular fire, causing casualties in the camps behind the siege works and forcing the battalions of La Sarre and Royal Roussillon to relocate to more protected positions. But the bombardment came at a price. Both the fort's 32-pdrs and an 18-pdr burst; three of the fort's most powerful guns destroyed before the French batteries had even opened fire. In desperation, Monro ordered the two 12-pdrs from the retrenchment into the fort.

The Indians maintained an annoying fire on the fort and camp all day, and rumours that British reinforcements were on the road brought a flurry

THE SIEGE OF FORT WILLIAM HENRY, 4–9 AUGUST 1757

Between 29 July and 3 August Montcalm moved his army, reduced to about 7,500 men, with 45 artillery pieces, from Fort Carillon, at the north end of Lake George, to invest Fort William Henry at the southern end. Having surrounded the fort he commenced siege operations on 4 August.

FRENCH FORCES

A Main French Camp (*c*.3,870 regulars, marines and *milice*)
B Lévis' Camp (*c*.2,060 *milice*)
C La Corne's Camp (*c*.1,600 Indians)
D Observation screen formed by Indians and Canadian *milice*

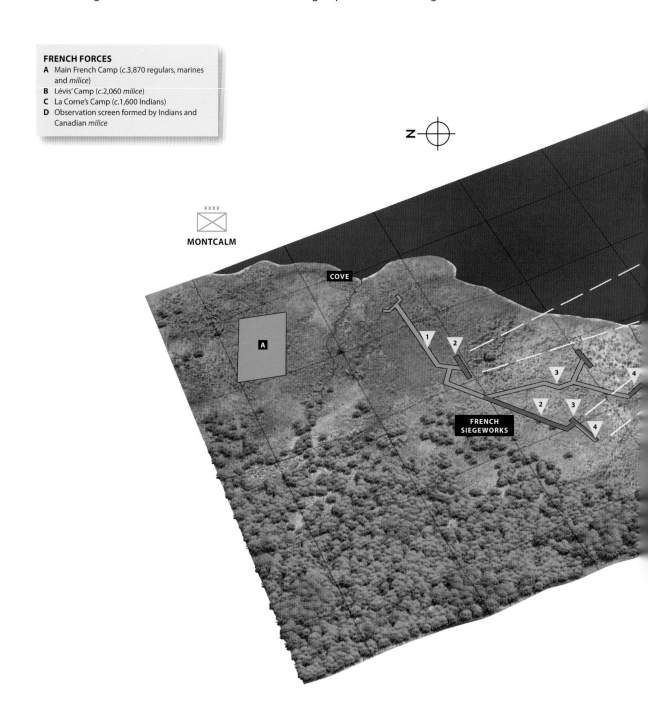

MONTCALM

COVE

A

FRENCH
SIEGEWORKS

Note: Gridlines are shown at intervals of 200m (218.7 yards)

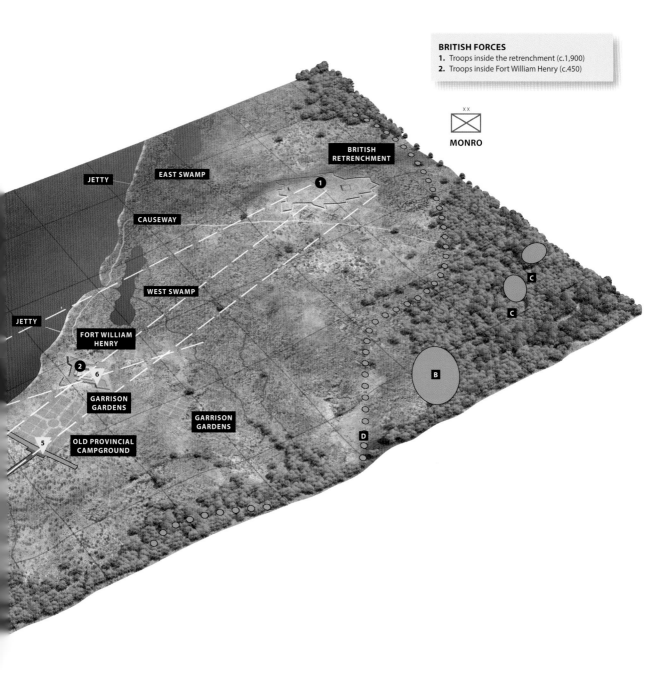

X X
MONRO

BRITISH RETRENCHMENT

EAST SWAMP

JETTY

CAUSEWAY

WEST SWAMP

JETTY

FORT WILLIAM HENRY

GARRISON GARDENS

GARRISON GARDENS

OLD PROVINCIAL CAMPGROUND

C

C

B

D

▼ EVENTS

1. 4 August: 800 French commence work on the first parallel, continuing right through the night, to link two batteries.

2. 5 August: work continues during the day on the left battery and improvements are made to the trench leading to the right battery. A thousand men work through the night to complete the left battery, install the artillery, and complete the trench leading to the right battery as well as continuing work on that battery.

3. 6 August: the left battery opens fire in the morning while work continues on the right battery. Five-hundred men work overnight completing the right battery and driving a trench forward.

4. 7 August: the right battery joins the left battery in action against fort and retrenched camp. Two-hundred men work through the day improving the trench started previous night. In the morning the French present Webb's intercepted letter to Monro. During the night the forward trench reaches a point about 200 yards from the fort. Work begins on a new parallel and battery.

5. 8 August: during the day a roadway is built across swampy ground for the movement of artillery. The second parallel extended and prepared for the construction of breaching batteries. Two-hundred men work overnight to improve the works completed during the day.

6. 9 August: Fort William Henry capitulates.

Throughout the siege Indians, individually and in groups, surrounded the fort and camp, keeping up a constant nagging fire on the defenders. On 7 August this sniping developed into an intense skirmish in which 21 Indians and *milice* were killed or wounded. (Photo courtesy of Katy Turle-Smith)

of activity, but it proved a false alarm. The British, however, were about to play right into Montcalm's hands.

A Caughnawaga Iroquois warrior named Kanectagon brought in a prisoner. Scouting out on the Fort Edward road he encountered three men. He killed one and captured another while the third escaped. They were the rangers carrying Webb's dismal letter to Monro. Kanectagon stripped the dead ranger of his bloodied coat and proudly took this booty and his prisoner back to the lake. French officers checking the coat discovered Webb's bloodstained letter. Montcalm recognized that it could hold the key to an early conclusion of the siege and that night significantly increased the work parties.

THE SIEGE – DAY 3 – WEBB WAITS

By the morning of 6 August the left battery was ready and the right battery neared completion. During the night straining teams dragged up eight cannon, including three 18-pdrs, and a 9in. mortar and positioned them in the battery. At 6.00am the first gun opened fire, quickly followed by the rest. The battery targeted the north-west bastion of the fort at a range of about 700 yards as well as the north wall and the shoreline of the lake where the two sloops lay. The position of the battery meant that any round overshooting the fort was likely to hit the camp. In this way a soldier of the Massachusetts Regiment 'had his thigh shot off … as he was standing sentry at Colonel Frye's tent door'. The French mortar proved effective too, wounding several of the garrison and damaging one of the fort's bronze 6-pdrs. Another shot ripped away the pulley of the flagstaff, causing the flag to flutter to the ground. French troops cheered vociferously at the symbolism. Two men managed to hoist the flag again but one 'had his head shot off with a ball' in the process. The artillery in the fort kept up a regular return fire on the battery but lost another 18-pdr and a 12-pdr, both bursting through overuse.

Back at Fort Edward, Webb briefly felt a glimmer of hope. On the morning of 6 August, Sir William Johnson rode in at the head of 180 Indians and about 1,500 militia, while another 46 Indians came in later. They joined those men who arrived on 4 August, rushed up from posts guarding the road to Albany. A constant stream of men followed throughout the day and the next. Later that day Webb had Bartman write a bullish note to Monro saying that he now had 5,000 men under his command and would 'set out in the night with the whole … and make no doubt of cutting the enemy entirely off'. But he didn't march. Perhaps realism set in. The majority of these men gathering at Fort Edward were untrained militia – farmers, shop keepers and labourers – they were no match for experienced French regulars and the supporting Canadians and Indians. Jabez Fitch, a sergeant in the Connecticut Regiment at Fort Edward, wrote in his diary on 7 August, 'we are impatient of waiting ... [but] we not yet strong enough to engage the enemy'.

History has damned Webb for not marching to Monro's aid – as did many of the provincial soldiers – but Loudoun had stripped New York of regular infantry to man his aborted campaign against Louisbourg. By nature a cautious man, Webb had received no information to counter the claim that an experienced army of 11,000 to 12,000 men were besieging Fort William Henry, or to tempt him into believing his hastily assembled force, the majority lacking proper military training, could be successful against them. He remained well aware that his own defeat could open the whole colony of New York to French incursion. And so he waited for his strength to increase further.

Back at Fort William Henry no written communication had got through to Monro since the French landed. Incredibly, two breathless rangers did get through to the embattled commander at about 2.00pm on 6 August and garbled out a verbal message relating to William Johnson. Unfortunately, Monro struggled to understand the meaning of their news, so incoherently did the messengers deliver it. Monro continued to wait for the assistance he believed must be coming.

French troops of the *Compagnies franches* line the siege works and keep up an irritating fire on the defenders of Fort William Henry to protect the working parties constructing the batteries.

THE SIEGE – DAY 4 – 'RELIEF IS GREATLY WANTED'

During the night of 6/7 August French working parties completed the right battery and installed 11 guns (two 18-pdrs, five 12-pdrs, one 8-pdr, two 7in. howitzers and a 6in. mortar). Having repaired damage inflicted during the day to the left battery these men also began driving a zigzag trench towards the fort.

At first light on 7 August the guns in the fort began to bombard both batteries. Montcalm appeared in the front line at 6.00am whereupon 'the two batteries received him with a general salute' and commenced a destructive fire on the fort and beyond to the camp. One of the beleaguered garrison wrote in his journal, 'This was the hottest days action from all quarters'. At about 9.00am the two French batteries halted their individual fire, then first one battery and then the other fired a salvo before falling silent. Having gained the attention of the fort's garrison the French raised a red flag to denote a parley. All guns ceased firing and an uneasy peace settled for a while on the southern shores of Lake George. It was time for Montcalm to play his trump card.

Montcalm's ADC, Bougainville, approached the fort and announced he had a letter for the British commander. Led blindfolded to Monro at his headquarters in the camp, Bougainville handed over a letter from Montcalm and with it Webb's letter intercepted two days earlier. Montcalm hoped that Monro, now facing bombardment from his siege batteries and made aware that help from Fort Edward remained doubtful, would accept the inevitable and surrender. Bougainville reported that Monro thanked him for his

IN THE FRENCH SIEGE LINES – FORT WILLIAM HENRY, AUGUST 1757 (PP. 72–73)

Montcalm's besieging French army commenced constructing their siege lines on 4 August and completed the Left Battery **(1)** during the night of 5/6 August. Guns of various calibres – 18-pdrs, 12-pdrs **(2)** and 8-pdrs as well as mortars and howitzers – had travelled up the lake secured to platforms fixed to pairs of bateaux and were placed in the battery that night. Recent research suggests that French artillery carriages changed from red to blue shortly after 1732. The guns in the Left Battery commenced firing on the morning of 6 August, the range to the fort's north-west bastion estimated at 700 yards. The guns were manned by the *Cannoniers-Bombardiers* **(3)**, the artillery arm raised in New France.

Father Roubaud, a Jesuit missionary to the Abenaki of St Francis, accompanied the warriors on the campaign against Fort William Henry and kept a detailed journal of all he saw. He noted the interest the Abenaki showed in the siege works. Fascinated by the digging, they 'examined the French Grenadiers with great curiosity as they built these works with the high degree of complexity they require. Learning with their eyes, they put this into practise. One would see them with picks and shovels, forming a new arm of the trench and lining it with rocks to fortify it, greatly reducing the strength of an attack.'

But the great artillery pieces attracted the attention of the Abenaki too as Roubaud explained. 'They were constantly around our gunners because they admired their dexterity. But their admiration was not passive. They wanted to try everything to make themselves more useful. They said they wished to become *cannoniers*; so they could distinguish themselves. After having fired a cannon for himself and hitting a corner of the fort one had achieved his goal.'**(4)** Impressed with his skill the French gunners tried to persuade him to try another shot but he refused. With his fellow warriors looking on with admiration **(5)** 'he said the reason for his refusal was that the first was so perfect he did not want to hazard the glory in a second attempt'.

politeness but added that he intended to continue the defence of his post. As soon as Bougainville regained the French lines the artillery opened up once more and 'a very hot fire ensued on both sides'.

Monro, although exasperated by the knowledge that Webb's letter had been in Montcalm's hands for two days, remained convinced that Webb would send help. On the morning of the following day he wrote, 'The fort and camp will hold out in hopes of the speedy relief from you which we hourly expect, and if that does not happen, we must fall into the hands of our enemies.' Then, in reference to the captured letter, he noted that it 'falling into [Montcalm's] hands was a very unhappy thing and has to be sure, elevated him greatly'. He finished the letter with a plea: 'Relief is greatly wanted.'

At the same time Webb was facing frustrations too, caused by the general dilatoriness of the militia. On 6 August he urged the commanders to make 'no unnecessary halts or delays' on their way to Fort Edward, adding, 'The firing still continues very heavy at Fort Wm. Henry. Pray God they may hold out till we can march to their assistance, but am afraid the delays of the Militia, will put it out of their or our power.'

A recreated barracks building at Fort William Henry. The garrison commander, Captain Ormsby, was seriously wounded by an exploding French shell while in the barrack block, forcing him to relinquish command. (Photo courtesy of Steve Vickers)

He wrote the following day too, asking the military officer at Albany to send urgent messages again to the militia colonels and provincial governors stating, 'That if they do not immediately order their respective militia to join the troops now here under the command of General Webb; this whole country must be deserted and given up to the enemy'.

Back at Lake George the ordinary fighting men had more immediate concerns. During the truce Louis Coulon de Villiers, a *Compagnies franches* officer commanding the 300 Canadian volunteers, took his men and a number of Indians around the east side of the camp under cover of a small knoll. They were now close to a position occupied by about 80 Massachusetts men. Seeing the French move, this detachment was reinforced by 200 men from Saltonstall's Massachusetts Company and Crookshanks' New York Independent Company. When the truce ended, a fierce and confusing firefight ensued which achieved nothing. At the end of it the British retired on their camp having 'lost several men, besides having several wounded'. Bougainville was scathing, reporting, 'We had 21 Indians and Canadians killed or wounded in this useless affair.'

The fort too was at the centre of the action. French cannon balls shattered the log walls and shells burst in the central parade ground and on the corner bastions. One shell exploding in a barrack building caused serious injury to Capt. Ormsby, the fort's commander. Inevitably two more of the fort's guns burst that day and French shells continued to cause injuries in the fort. Dragged down into the dark casemates under the barracks, the wounded joined the other patients, amongst who were many suffering from smallpox.

The events of the day caused Monro to take steps to prevent defeatism taking hold in the fort. He issued an order stating that, 'If any person proved cowardly or offered to advise giving up the Fort that he should be immediately hanged over the walls.' Even so, that night shots rang out as two British deserters made for the French lines under cover of darkness. The gunfire brought forth piercing whoops of approval from Indian encampments in the surrounding mountains. It did nothing to boost fading morale.

THE SIEGE – DAY 5 – THE END DRAWS NEAR

Through the rest of the night of 7/8 August the French pushed a trench forward into marshy sunken ground and began a new battery in advance of the first. At daylight they laid fascines across the marshy ground and placed logs on top to form a roadway for the artillery. From the fort the guns continued to batter the works but their constant losses greatly reduced their effectiveness. The return fire from the French batteries 'did great damage both in the fort and camp'. The French continued digging through the daylight hours and, during the night of 8/9 August, worked their way up out of the marshy area and commenced a new parallel at the edge of the fort's garden. From here they would add the breaching batteries. Conscious of the threat, the fort's guns maintained a heavy fire on the works all through the night, which Bougainville recorded 'had never been so lively'.

There had been a scare for the French during the day when reports arrived announcing that a British relief force had finally marched from Fort Edward. Montcalm ordered a strong force out to intercept them but it proved another false alarm.

After the constant pounding suffered by the fort during the day, Monro sent in an engineer to assess the damage. His report was stark; it concluded that the fort was almost defenceless and the garrison exhausted after four nights with little or no sleep. Monro called a council of war for the morning.

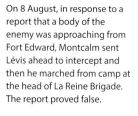

On 8 August, in response to a report that a body of the enemy was approaching from Fort Edward, Montcalm sent Lévis ahead to intercept and then he marched from camp at the head of La Reine Brigade. The report proved false.

While things were looking desperate at Lake George, at Fort Edward Brigadier-General Webb's force was gradually growing. In a letter dispatched to Monro at 6.00pm, Webb's ADC explained 'that it is entirely owing to the delay of the Militia that he has not yet mov'd up to your assistance, but as he has now got a party of them and expects a thousand more tomorrow, you may depend, on their arrival, that he will not fail to march to your assistance'.

Yet three days later Webb wrote to Lord Loudoun stating he had just 4,500 men fit for service on the day of the capitulation. The French intercepted Webb's latest letter to Monro the following day and passed it to him. A French officer, the Comte de Malartic, reported that 'the British officers complain loudly', because by then it was too late; Monro had surrendered.

THE SIEGE – DAY 6 – SURRENDER

At break of day on 9 August the garrison's situation looked bleak. The new parallel completed overnight ran just 200 yards from the walls of the fort at its closest point. A concentrated bombardment from that range would reduce the log walls to matchwood. When another gun then burst, a quick inventory revealed just five (a 9-pdr, two 6-pdrs and two 4-pdrs) of the original 17 cannon remained serviceable, along with a mortar and howitzer.

The council of war, having considered their situation and the unlikelihood of relief from Fort Edward, agreed to seek honourable surrender terms. At about 7.00am Monro ordered a white flag hoisted over the fort.

The terms of surrender proved generous. Montcalm offered the full honours of war. The officers and men would retain their personal baggage and return to Fort Edward under escort, taking with them a 6-pdr as a mark of their gallant defence, and Montcalm undertook to care for any of the sick and wounded unable to march. In return Monro agreed that the garrison would not serve against France or her allies for 18 months and accepted a clause agreeing to the return of all French, Canadian and Indian prisoners taken since the war began. Other than the 6-pdr, Montcalm would take possession of all artillery, vessels, munitions and provisions, although the men retained their muskets but not their ammunition.

It was of course in Montcalm's power to take the garrison prisoner but he had to be pragmatic. Food and supplies were limited at the best of times in New France; a requirement to feed more than 2,000 extra mouths for an indefinite period was an unwanted and impractical burden, better to take the garrison out of the war and let the British feed and supply their own.

Before the capitulation could be signed, though, Montcalm, mindful of the actions of his Indian allies after the surrender of Oswego, felt it necessary to inform them what was about to happen. During the negotiations Indians had already moved freely around the fort and camp and walked off with the few remaining horses belonging to the garrison. Now, Montcalm was about to explain the formalities of 18th-century siege warfare to the leaders of 18 Indian nations through the words of three missionaries, ten interpreters and the 16 officers assigned to them.

Early on the morning of 9 August, Rudolphus Faesch, a French-speaking captain of the Royal Americans, marched out with a small escort to inform Montcalm that the garrison was ready to negotiate terms of surrender.

Until Monro raised the white flag, Montcalm's Indian allies understood that the siege guns were about to batter a breach in the fort's walls. A French account reported that the warriors 'had applied to mount the breach with the grenadiers and were waiting with impatience for the moment to do so'. What they now heard made no sense. Everything for which they had travelled so far lay in the fort and camp, but now they were to stand by while their defeated enemies marched away unhindered, carrying all their property with them. At a council of all the Indian leaders Montcalm informed them of the articles granted to the besieged garrison and asked for their consent, which they reportedly gave, although no one could know exactly how the interpreters translated his words. He then asked the leaders to restrain their young warriors and ensure they adhered to the agreement. It was a step further than Montcalm had taken at Oswego but it seems naïve of him to think that a few words would convince his Indian allies to return home with no reward to show for their victorious campaign. Even so, those present indicated their acceptance and Monro signed the formal surrender at noon on 9 August; the six-day siege was over. The British had lost 45 men killed and 70 wounded during the gallant defence; the French recorded their losses as only 13 killed and 40 wounded.

ABANDONING THE FORT

Even as a brief handover ceremony took place, numbers of Indians swarmed into the fort through the gun embrasures 'searching in every nook and corner' for booty. They found little. One provincial officer reported they, 'began to plunder many small things as – brass kettles, etc., etc.' Then, even as the garrison marched off to the camp, haunting screams were heard from inside the fort. In the casemates disgruntled warriors had discovered those too sick or injured to march, and, as the Jesuit missionary Roubaud described it, 'these were the victims upon whom they piteously rushed'. Describing the stench emanating from the casemate as 'insupportable', as he looked around he saw a grinning warrior emerge from the noxious cavern. In his hand he carried 'a human head, from which trickled streams of blood, and which he displayed as the most splendid prize that he could have secured'. Then French regulars intervened, putting a stop to any more killing and prevented the Indians taking the provisions and munitions. Frustrated in the fort, some Indians turned their attention to the cemetery and began disinterring bodies to take the scalps and clothing of the dead as their prizes. It was here that the smallpox victims lay buried.

The march from the fort to the camp was intimidating for

The low roof marks the entrance to the casemate built under the east barracks. These barracks did not feature in the reconstruction but excavations revealed part of the casemate. The slaughter of many of the sick and wounded took place here.

the garrison. Warriors crowded along the route 'eyeing the passengers backwards and forwards, very narrowly'. One of the men reported that the Indians 'laugh'd and made considerable fun of us as we march'd along, well knowing, the property of our packs, would remain with us but a very short time'.

However, the ordeal did not end when they reached the camp. Although the French had detailed a guard of about 200 men, the constant probes by the Indians all around the perimeter meant it was impossible to prevent them entering the camp to pilfer. The situation became tense. The reputation of the Indian warriors as ruthless and barbaric killers was well established amongst the British and colonial soldiers, and there was a general reluctance to antagonize them as they stalked around the camp that afternoon, proving themselves 'very troublesome'. There were concerns about the amount of alcohol in the camp; the Indians went on the rampage at Oswego after finding the garrison's rum supply. Recognizing the problem, Monro ordered the immediate disposal of all alcohol at a regimental level. Whether every individual soldier disposed of personal supplies is open to question.

The view looking back from the retrenchment towards the fort about 600 yards away. Many French cannon balls that overshot the fort landed in the camp.

As the afternoon wore on the Indians became bolder and turned their attention to the officers' baggage. Some offered money to secure their belongings but an air of menace increased. There were civilians in camp too, men, women and children. For them the situation became terrifying.

In the afternoon, as tensions in the camp came close to boiling over, Montcalm arrived and only after his 'entreaties, threats, flattery, conferences with the chiefs, the intervention of officers and interpreters who have any authority over these barbarians' was some form of order restored. In his journal entry for that day Bougainville, having observed the simmering tensions, solemnly wrote, 'We will be most fortunate if we can avoid a massacre.' Initially Montcalm recommended to Monro that he bring his departure forward from the following morning to that night to avoid any further issues with the Indians. He informed Monro that he would provide an escort of 200 regular infantry drawn from the Béarn and Languedoc regiments as well as the 500 men of the *Compagnies franches* brigade. However, only at 9.00pm did the situation appear sufficiently quiet to enable Montcalm to retire to his own camp and therefore he recommended a delay in departure of over 24 hours to allow the 'passion of the Indians' to subside.

Monro, however, wanted to get away. He told Montcalm he wished to march his men out of the camp at midnight and asked for the promised escort. Later that night one of those in the camp reported that 'with great silence we got under arms'. With the grenadier company of the 35th at the front the column began to form but the escort did not appear. An hour later a message arrived from Montcalm. He had information that as many as two-thirds of his Indians were not in their camps; he presumed they were planning to ambush the British column. In the circumstances he advised Monro to delay his departure until morning. For any watching Indians this must have appeared disconcerting. Were the French colluding with their enemies and

THE 'MASSACRE', 10 AUGUST 1757 (PP. 80–81)

When Lt. Col. Monro surrendered Fort William Henry (1) to Montcalm on 9 August, the attitude of the French allied Indians was very much on the minds of both commanders. Through interpreters Montcalm explained the terms to the Indian leaders and asked their acceptance. These amounted to granting the garrison the full honours of war and allowing them to march away with all their personal property. That the Indian leaders appeared to accept these terms should have concerned Montcalm more than it did, because if they adhered to the agreement it meant they had fought the campaign for nothing, gaining neither booty, scalps, prisoners or the chance to prove themselves as warriors.

Throughout the afternoon of 9 August warriors infiltrated the British camp, grabbing what they wanted, the soldiers and civilians advised not to antagonize them by refusing or resisting.

The following morning, as the British column prepared to march out, many Indians reappeared, grabbing what they could and attacking the wounded. The feeling of unease amongst the British intensified.

The column eventually moved off on the road (2) to Fort Edward, with the British regulars leading, followed by the provincial regiments then the civilians. More Indians now appeared and the snatching and jostling escalated until, above the growing disorder at the back of the column, a warrior gave the war whoop and suddenly the killing began.

Disorder and confusion spread rapidly up the column, some men halted, others broke and ran to join other groups, some fled. With the scattering of the column the fierceness of the killing slowed down as the warriors' attention turned to preventing valuable prisoners escaping.

Here a small group, an officer and two men of the 35th Regiment (3), joined by a soldier of the 60th Regiment (4) and one from a provincial regiment (5), do their best to protect themselves. Most have lost items of clothing, which were highly prized by their Indian attackers. Another man, a provincial, having suffered similarly makes a desperate dash (6) to join them. Jonathan Carver, a soldier in the Massachusetts provincials, escaping from his Indian captors made for a group such as this, regained his breath then sprinted for the woods and, eventually, reached safety at Fort Edward. Elsewhere other warriors are taking scalps and prisoners (7).

helping them to march away under cover of darkness, carrying away the property they felt was their reward for service in the campaign?

The British returned to camp. As the soldiers and civilians settled uncomfortably around their campfires, few slept. Many pondered the fate of those left behind in the fort, while experienced frontiersmen no doubt recounted lurid stories to younger soldiers of Indian atrocities in years gone by. And every now and then unearthly Indian yells pierced the night, hinting at untold horrors lurking in the shadows. One provincial officer recalled, 'All the remainder of this night the Indians were in great numbers round our lines and seemed to show more than usual malice in their looks which made us suspect they intended us mischief.'

THE 'MASSACRE'

The long, dark, threatening hours of night eventually gave way to the early morning light and the unhappy garrison prepared to depart once more. Monro formed them up within the retrenchment but already Indians were appearing around the lines of the camp. Montcalm had provided an overnight guard but it was impossible to prevent the Indians crossing the breastwork at any convenient point. The commander of the Massachusetts Regiment, Col. Frye, watched them move freely about the camp and felt that they appeared 'in a worse temper (if possible) than last night', and noted warily that each carried 'a tomahawk, hatchet, or some other instrument of death'.

The unwelcome visitors soon began making aggressive demands and the officers' baggage particularly attracted close attention again. Jonathan Carver, a sergeant in the Massachusetts Regiment, reported that they hoped the Indians would be satisfied with this plunder and 'suffered them to proceed without opposition. Indeed it was not in our power to make any, had we been so inclined; for though we were permitted to carry off our arms, yet we were not allowed a single round of ammunition'. But Carver's hopes quickly faded.

As a sergeant in the Massachusetts Regiment, Jonathan Carver survived the Indian attack and left a fascinating account of his experiences that day in his book, *Travels Through the Interior Parts of North America*, published in 1813.

A section of the camp nearby served as a rudimentary hospital administered by Miles Whitworth, a surgeon attached to the Massachusetts Regiment. He had 17 sick men who were unable to march and these had officially come under French care the previous afternoon. A guard placed on the hospital marched off at 5.00am leaving Whitworth alone with his charges. He looked on helplessly as a group of Indians dragged the sick men out of their huts to 'murder them with their tomahawks and scalp them'. He reported that a number of Canadian officers and French troops were close by but did nothing to prevent the killings.

Elsewhere, once inside the camp lines, the Indians homed in on black and Indian soldiers serving in the rangers or provincial regiments. Hauling out the Indians with 'great fierceness', the warriors singled some out and viciously 'cut them to pieces'; others, including the black soldiers, they led off. The Indians understood the European concept of blacks as property and claimed them as booty.

As the French escort marched up, Lt. Col. Monro complained about the blatant disregard of the terms of the capitulation. Realizing there was little he could do to curtail the Indians' avarice, the officer commanding the escort

The site of the hospital huts within the British camp. On the morning of 10 August the 17 patients were dragged out and hacked to death by Indians seeking scalps and booty. (Photo courtesy of Steve Vickers)

advised Monro to give up the baggage and the men's packs, believing it would quell their demands. Monro consented and 'ordered every man to throw down his baggage, which was soon convey'd away'.

Those Indians who had secured booty, be it scalps, prisoners or plunder, were now returning to their woodland bivouacs. Suddenly alerted, others poured out of the camps determined not to miss out on their share of the spoils.

Monro had by now begun to march from the camp, leading with the Royal Artillery and 35th Regiment at the front of the column. The Indians had already that morning made off with the horses provided to pull the 6-pdr granted to the garrison in recognition of its gallant defence. The men of the 60th Regiment formed up next. Now the bolder of the newly arrived Indians began snatching and clawing at the soldiers as they tried to march away, grabbing at 'hats, swords, guns, and clothes, stripping them all to their shirts, and on some officers left no shirt at all'. One of those officers felt powerless and wished 'our selves in the same situation, we were in before the Capitulation; thinking to fight as long as we could and at last die like soldiers; preferable to the shocking brutality, wherewith the Savages treated us'.

As his regiment left the retrenchment, Carver was grabbed by three or four Indians who tore away his clothing and personal possessions, leaving him with just his breeches and shirt when he broke free. (Photo courtesy of Leslea Barnes Photography)

Another caught up in the horror later recalled that the officers did all they could to keep their men calm, advising them not to resist and give up to the Indians what they demanded so that none 'should fall a sacrifice to their unbounded fury'. To stress their continued adherence to the terms of surrender, those soldiers who still retained their muskets were ordered to carry them clubbed, a motion confirming surrender. It seems unlikely, though, that those born in the forests of North America would recognize this nicety of European military etiquette.

The provincial regiments brought up the rear of the column, with the camp followers marching last of all. As the numbers in the camp reduced, those remaining now attracted the full attention of the Indians still lurking inside. Colonel Frye recorded that his men left the camp with some difficulty. Carver described how, as he approached the camp gateway, three or four Indians grabbed him. With weapons held threateningly above his head, others, he recalled, 'disrobed me of my coat, waistcoat, hat, and buckles, omitting not to take from me what money I had in my pocket'. Carver broke free and sought protection from a French soldier near the gateway, but he claimed the guard pushed him away, calling him an English dog. Looking around he saw a few men of his regiment crowded together some distance away and made a dash to join them. On the way 'innumerable were the blows' that struck him, including spear thrusts to his side and ankle.

The civilians brought up the rear of the column and were amongst the first to be attacked when the war whoop sounded and the killing began. Men, women and children, all considered equal targets, 'were despatched in the most wanton and cruel manner'. (Photo courtesy of Leslea Barnes Photography)

Once the last elements of the column scrambled from the camp the situation rapidly deteriorated further. The tail of the column, far behind the French escort that formed near the head of the column, and made up of men of the New Hampshire Regiment and the terrified camp followers, now began to be harassed even more violently than before; then, above the shouts of protest and cries of anguish, the 'hell whoop' sounded. A French source attributes the signal to the 36 Abenaki warriors from Panaomeska. Emboldened by the absence of any physical resistance, the Abenaki unleashed a murderous assault. Carver, who had reached temporary safety, watched and recalled that 'the Indians began to murder those that were nearest to them without distinction … men, women and children were despatched in the most wanton and cruel manner, and immediately scalped'.

Father Roubaud, who arrived as this killing broke out, wrote, 'This butchery, which in the beginning was the work of only a few Savages, was the signal which made nearly all of them so many ferocious beasts. They struck, right and left, heavy blows of the hatchet on those who fell into their hands.'

Those at the front of the column, unsure as to what was happening at the rear, were ordered to halt, which, Colonel Frye reported, 'was done in great confusion'. Moments later, when it became clear that the rear was under attack, the leading elements 'again pressed forward, and thus the confusion continued and increased'. Any sense of the column as a military formation ended.

In the confusion British officers sought out their French counterparts from the escort demanding protection for their men. Many of them, however, overwhelmed by this sudden escalation, felt helpless and unable to intercede. They advised the British 'to take to the woods and shift for themselves'. Many were already doing so. An officer with the artillery reported, 'all efforts proved ineffectual to prevent their running away in a very confused and irregular manner'.

Father Roubaud, a witness of events as they unfolded, observed that once the killings began it made the warriors 'so many ferocious beasts. They struck, right and left, heavy blows of the hatchet on those who fell into their hands.'

As the column disintegrated so the initial frenzy of killing subsided. Father Roubaud wrote, with a little relief, that 'the massacre was not of long continuance, or so great as such fury gave us cause to fear; the number of men killed was hardly more than forty or fifty'.

With the column breaking up valuable prisoners were now escaping. Mindful that at Oswego the French had paid handsomely to recover prisoners taken by them, the Indians' priority now turned to capturing as many of the desperate, fleeing men as they could. And desperate they were.

Carver, having escaped one close encounter, now found himself in an isolated clump of about 20 men from his own regiment. Seeing no better option they decided to make 'one vigorous effort' to break through the Indians. Carver ran and managed to push over some surprised would-be assailants while others he dodged past, 'dextrously avoiding their weapons', until two stout Indians grabbed him whose grip he could not shake free. Carver felt sure his captors were about to kill him. But, at that moment an officer wearing just his fine velvet breeches dashed by, at which one of his captors released his grip on Carver and tried to seize this new quarry. Surprisingly the officer threw his attacker to the ground and was about to get away when Carver's other captor released him too. Instantly Carver dashed away, but as he cast a glance behind him he saw 'the Indian's tomahawk gash into [the officer's] back, and heard him utter his last groan'. After further narrow escapes and three days and nights wandering through the rugged forest, Carver eventually reached safety at Fort Edward. Not everyone was so lucky.

FRENCH TROOPS REGAIN CONTROL

The French escort finally began to assert itself when Lévis appeared. Confrontations with their Indian allies resulted in the death of one soldier of the escort and three wounded as they began to restore order. As soon as Montcalm heard of the disturbances he hurried to the scene with a number of other officers. There was no time to form the regiments to march. By the time he arrived the killing frenzy was over and the Indians were gathering prisoners. Having secured Monro and those men closest to him, Father Roubaud watched as Montcalm then attempted to reclaim prisoners from their captors, using 'prayers, menaces, promises'. When that failed he resorted to force. Roubaud saw Montcalm rescue a nephew of Lt. Col. Young from the hands of his captor 'with authority and with violence'. Others, seeing Montcalm's actions and fearing the loss of their own captives, 'immediately massacred' them, taking their scalps instead.

The belated vigorous action by Montcalm, Lévis and others secured between 400 and 500 of the British. But many others remained captive and, determined they would not have their prizes taken from them, most Indians left the army that same day; they had what they had come for. By the end of the day only the Abenaki and Nipissing remained – fewer than 300 warriors. Montcalm knew too that the *milice* needed to depart for home to bring in the vital harvest without which New France might starve. Without Indian and Canadian support the campaign was over.

As soon as he became aware of what was happening, Montcalm rushed to the scene with a group of officers and used whatever means possible to retake captives from his Indian allies. This caused many to scalp their captives rather than lose them to the French.

AFTERMATH

At Fort Edward they received the first news of the capitulation at about 8.00pm on 9 August, brought in by a Frenchman serving in the ranks of the Massachusetts Regiment who thought it prudent to abscond as soon as the surrender was confirmed. Webb put Fort Edward on full alert and then, between 9.00am and 10.00am the following morning, the first group of about 30 breathless survivors staggered in bringing with them colours of the 35th Regiment. Behind them, some time later, followed the largest single group that escaped the Indians' attack. Bewildered, battered, breathless and stripped of clothing and weapons, these men recounted their disjointed stories to the wide-eyed garrison at Fort Edward, telling of massacre and bloody murder, of atrocities seen and imagined amongst the confusion of the moment. Stories circulated rapidly around the camps, embellished with every telling. They told of women horrendously killed, babies torn from their mother's arms and their heads smashed against rocks. Then these stories travelled quickly along the roads of New York before spreading to the neighbouring New England colonies.

Webb ordered that a cannon be fired every two hours to help guide in any survivors still lost in the woods. Colonel Frye staggered in during the night of 11/12 August. Sergeant Carver eventually arrived on 13 August. There were others too. Webb heard from some of these survivors that Monro was under French protection, but no word came from Montcalm. Somewhat surprisingly French deserters also appeared at Fort Edward. They informed Webb that Montcalm planned to destroy Fort William Henry. About noon on 11 August a large column of smoke appeared in the sky confirming their story. They also brought the welcome news that the Indians had left the army, reassuring the unsettled commander that the chances of any further French advance were diminishing.

Four days after the attack around 600 survivors had gathered at Fort Edward, fuelling rumours that the Indian attack had killed or taken prisoner up to 1,700 of the garrison.

A skull recovered during the archaeological investigation of the Fort William Henry site in the 1950s. It is believed that the large crack in the cranium is the result of a heavy strike from a tomahawk. (Photo courtesy of the Fort William Henry Museum)

The estimates of those killed multiplied with each telling of the survivors' stories. But on the evening of 14 August, Montcalm finally sent word that he held Monro and about 500 officers, soldiers and civilians and that they would be marched under escort towards Fort Edward the following day. Having held them for five days, a French report claimed that Montcalm 'retained the English he had recovered … to allow the fury of the Indians to die out'. But most of the warriors had departed on 10 August. It seems a strange decision, yet there is a suggestion that Montcalm, using modern parlance, retained them as a human shield. Montcalm treated them well but he benefited from their presence; they would be useful if Webb threatened to attack while the demolition of Fort William Henry was underway. He sent them back on the day the work was completed.

On a personal level the outcome of the surrender continued to dismay Montcalm, even though publicly the French blamed the victims for some of the responsibility for their fate, suggesting they gave the Indians alcohol – an accusation Monro vehemently denied – and refused to defend themselves. Determined not to have himself cast as the villain, Montcalm sent word to Vaudreuil at Montréal to intercept any Indians with prisoners. Many were happy to sell, but to ensure the best price they first focused French attention by killing one 'in the presence of the entire town … put him in a kettle, and forced his unfortunate compatriots to eat him'. After lengthy negotiations the French secured most of these prisoners, leaving the Indians to rejoice in the European riches of clothing, tobacco, vermilion, lace and brandy by the keg.

A group of skeletons discovered during excavations of the casemate under the east barracks of Fort William Henry. Here the wounded and sick were attacked by Indians after the surrender of the fort. (Photo courtesy of the Fort William Henry Museum)

Many also took back a far less welcome gift to their villages – smallpox. The disease would devastate whole communities that year.

Subsequent research[1] estimates that by the end of 1757, of the paroled garrison the fate of just 308 soldiers remained unclear, plus an unknown number of civilians. But by the end of the Seven Years' War in 1763 the conclusion this research draws is that perhaps only 174 soldiers were unaccounted for – either killed in the massacre or amongst those taken away by the Indians and not sold back to the French, who, adopted into Indian families, lived out their lives in distant Indian villages across Canada. The exact number killed in the 'massacre' will never be known accurately but on 15 August, when Monro and the rest of those rescued by the French marched back to Fort Edward, they reported what they saw on the road. It amounted to 'Near 30 carcasses ... and from the frequent stenches they met, had reason to imagine many more lay scattered about.' When you add in those butchered in the hospital earlier that morning, far from it being a wholesale slaughter, perhaps the total killed in the 'massacre' by up to 1,600 warriors was restricted to between 50 and 80 victims.

So, while the extent of the Fort William Henry 'massacre' of classic fiction and Hollywood is overplayed, there can be no doubt that at the time it had a profound effect on the colonists of America. And for those caught up in the fury of the Indian attack, brief though it may have been, and those who endured terrifying mental torture as prisoners, not knowing if they were to be killed at any moment, it became an indelible nightmare, haunting the survivors for the rest of their lives and entering the psyche of a nation.

SUMMARY

The campaign of 1757 proved a disaster for the British. Loudoun, having concentrated his regular troops for an attack against Louisbourg, aborted the attack when he received news that three French naval squadrons had reached the fortress; this enforced absence of troops now left the New York frontier vulnerable to attack. While Loudoun was at sea Montcalm successfully attacked and captured Fort William Henry but lacked the resources to penetrate deeper into New York.

Brigadier General Webb, senior officer on the New York frontier, was not a dynamic leader of men and held a low opinion of the fighting qualities of the local troops. With limited manpower the strategic risks in moving to support Monro at Fort William Henry were great – if he met with defeat. Webb's request to the colonial governors to call out the militia did not reach the governor of New York until the evening of 3 August; by then the French had already surrounded the fort. Webb complained bitterly about the tardiness of the militia to march to his support, yet in reality, the late call to arms and the great distances involved were always going to delay the arrival of the militia on the frontier. Yet even had they been on hand earlier, how would largely untrained militia have fared when confronted by experienced regular soldiers and Indian warriors at home in the forest and keen to display their prowess in battle? Webb's confidence appeared to ebb and flow during this period and he found himself pilloried for his caution; some muttered

---

1 See *Betrayals: Fort William Henry & the 'Massacre'*, Ian K. Steele, New York, 1990.

accusations of cowardice. That Montcalm retired after destroying Fort William Henry meant Webb's resolve was not tested in battle.

Lieutenant-Colonel Monro, in his first active command, conducted a stout defence of Fort William Henry but remained deeply affected by the outcome of the capitulation. Posted to Albany after his release, Monro collapsed in the street on 3 November and died, his death attributed to apoplexy (stroke). In January 1758, before news of his death reached London, he was gazetted a full colonel.

Although London subsequently recalled Loudoun and Webb, both avoided any official criticism and received promotions. Loudoun became lieutenant-general and fought against the Spanish in 1762 before becoming a full general in 1770. Webb received promotion to major-general in 1759 and lieutenant-general two years later. But amongst his peers his performance in North America continued to dog him through the rest of his career.

In 1758 the British Army in North America was under new management. It met with mixed results. Early in July, Montcalm inflicted a heavy defeat on the British at Fort Carillon. But the victory proved to be the high-water mark for New France because later that month the surrender of Louisbourg opened the doors to Québec and the dramatic capture of that city the following year. At Québec, Montcalm led the French Army for the last time. As he lay mortally wounded amidst the ruins of the shattered city, New France, largely abandoned by the mother country, twisted agonizingly in its death throes. The British Army had learnt the ways of war in North America.

THE BATTLEFIELD TODAY

The reconstructed Fort William Henry stands in very different surroundings today than its predecessor did back in the 18th century. What was once virgin forest is now the thriving holiday resort of Lake George Village in upstate New York. There is no doubt that, on a hot summer's day with the shimmering blue lake nestling at the foot of the imposing Adirondack mountains, it is a beautiful spot.

Although Montcalm razed the original fort straight after the siege, the mounds and bumps marking the outline of the original site remained visible into the 20th century. But as tourism expanded around the lake and the site came under threat from development, two local businessmen purchased the land to protect it. Archaeological work then began and in 1953 a plan was approved to reconstruct the fort. Despite an enforced closure following an arson attack in 1967, which seriously damaged part of the fort, it has remained open (May–September) ever since.

The cemetery outside Fort William Henry under archaeological excavation in the 1950s. Some Indians resorted to exhuming bodies in the cemetery in their search for plunder. Amongst the dead were recent victims of smallpox. Those warriors unwittingly carried the virus back to their home villages with devastating results for the Native American people. (Photo courtesy of the Fort William Henry Museum)

The reconstructed fort is built, more or less, on the original footprint, and while it does not use period construction techniques it still creates a good impression of the appearance of the original fort. It is family orientated, with guided tours, musket, grenade and cannon-firing demonstrations, and has a museum showing many of the original artefacts unearthed during the ongoing archaeological digs.

While the area where Montcalm's main force encamped during the siege has long since disappeared under the sprawl of bars, restaurants and shops of Lake George Village, there is a marker in Lower Montcalm Street to show the site.

The area of swampy ground to the east of the fort which influenced the battle has long been drained and now forms Lake George Battlefield Park. Here an impressive statue of General Johnson and the Mohawk sachem Theyanoguin commemorates the 1755 battle of Lake George. A little further to the east of the statue is the rising ground on which Johnson anchored his position during that battle and a marker shows where four soldiers killed in the 'Bloody Morning Scout' were later buried after being disinterred during road construction. This same piece of raised ground is the position where the British hastily built the retrenched camp in the final days before Montcalm commenced the siege of Fort William Henry. At the north end of this raised ground stands a sign marking the location of the 'hospital' during the siege, whose inmates were amongst the first killed by the Indians on the day of the 'massacre'.

A couple of miles south of Lake George, on Route 9, you can find other reminders of the battle of Lake George – Bloody Pond and the monument to Col. Ephraim Williams.

And, if after all that exploring you'd like to take things easy, there is always one of the cruises on the lake, which regularly take passengers as far as the Narrows, thus completing your overview of the campaign area.

FURTHER READING

Bradfield, G. E., *Fort William Henry – Digging up History* (New York, 2001)

Hamilton, E. P., ed., *Adventure in the Wilderness: The American Journals of Louis Antoine de Bougainville, 1756–1760* (Oklahoma, 1990)

Hughes, B., *The Siege of Fort William Henry – A Year on the Northeastern Frontier* (Yardley, Penn., 2011)

Parkman, F., *Montcalm and Wolfe: The French & Indian War* (New York, 1995 reprint)

Starbuck, D. R., *Massacre at Fort William Henry* (Lebanon, NH, 2002)

Steele, I. K., *Betrayals: Fort William Henry and the 'Massacre'* (New York, 1990)

For those seeking access to primary sources I strongly recommend the online 'Internet Archive', www.archive.org. The following proved particularly useful during the preparation of this book.

Carver, J., *Travels Through the Interior Parts of North America* (Walpole, NH, 1813)

Hays, I. M., *A Journal Kept During the Siege of Fort William Henry, August 1757* (1898)

O'Callaghan, E. B., and Bertold Fernow, eds., *Documents Relative to the Colonial History of the State of New York, Vol. 6, London Documents* (Albany, NY, 1853–87)

O'Callaghan, E. B., and Bertold Fernow, eds., *Documents Relative to the Colonial History of the State of New York, Vol. 10, Paris Documents* (Albany, NY, 1853–87)

Pargellis, S., ed., *Military Affairs in North America, 1748–65: Selected Documents from the Cumberland Papers in Windsor Castle* (New York, 1936)

Putnam, R., *Journal of Gen. Rufus Putnam Kept in Northern New York During Four Campaigns of the Old French and Indian War, 1757–1760,* (Albany, NY, 1886)

Scull, G. D., *The Montresor Journals* (New York, 1882)

Sullivan, J., Flick, A. C., Hamilton, M. W., Corey, A., eds., *The Papers of Sir William Johnson, Vol. 2* (Albany, NY, 1921)

Thwaites, R. G., ed., *The Jesuit Relations and Allied Documents: Travels and Explorations of the Jesuit Missionaries in New France, 1610–1791 (Vol.70)* (Cleveland, 1896–1901)

INDEX